Gift ✓

D0330893

Making
the Ministry
Relevant

Making
the Ministry
Relevant

EDITED BY HANS HOFMANN

DIRECTOR, THE HARVARD UNIVERSITY PROJECT ON

RELIGION AND MENTAL HEALTH

CHARLES SCRIBNER'S SONS · NEW YORK

WINGATE COLLEGE LIBRARY
WINGATE, N. C.

Copyright © 1960 Charles Scribner's Sons

"*The Christian Moral Witness and Some Disciplines of Modern Culture*" copyright © 1960 Reinhold Niebuhr

The passage on p. 91 taken from Thornton Wilder's *The Woman of Andros* (published by A. C. Boni) is used with kind permission of the author

This book published simultaneously in the
United States of America and in Canada—
Copyright under the Berne Convention

All rights reserved. No part of this book
may be reproduced in any form without the
permission of Charles Scribner's Sons.

Printed in the United States of America

LIBRARY OF CONGRESS CATALOG CARD NUMBER 60-14020

To Ed and Betty Welles

51466

INTRODUCTION

IT IS a common assumption that the ministry possesses a perpetually valid message without regard to the changing contours of history. The title of this book implies the contrary assumption. The implication is not that the Christian faith and what it stands for have become highly questionable and need therefore a plea of defense for its very reason of existence; nor that the Christian faith and the ministry of the church should be offered under a new name or in a more palatable form, thereby selling short their unique character. Rather, the assumption is that the Christian faith is highly relevant and its ministry has a significant place and function in our culture and time. The crucial point is whether we have been slow in recognizing the real potency of our faith and hence inefficient in our ministry.

The term ministry comes from the Latin word for service. The question is therefore whom do we serve and how do we serve Him. The Judeo-Christian tradition has always spoken of that strange God who is not satisfied with enjoying Himself far away from the tribulations of His human creatures and the problems into which they maneuver themselves so skillfully. The Bible speaks of God as someone who becomes of His own free will the servant of man, even in human form and among human beings on earth. The deity becomes the suffering servant and the one persecuted and executed by the pious and mighty ones.

When we speak of serving God we mean attuning ourselves to His hidden ways of seeking out those who need and welcome His help. Serving God means serving men where and whenever it dawns on them that all they could do for themselves and by themselves will not really solve the fundamental question as to how one can be human in a given time and cultural setting. It might well be that God in His strange and hidden way prods people here and there to ask questions beyond the practical considerations of their daily lives, forcing them to concentrate on the meaning and purpose of existence.

In our period it is the social sciences and the growing knowledge in psychotherapy which make it obvious that it is not enough for human beings to be secure, successful and enjoying a high standard of living. Every human being has the innate and irrepressible urge to make sense of life and to have this sense expressed through the unique character of his own personality and in the precise context in which he lives and works. To serve people in the name of God requires that we be able to recognize and understand this urge. We need to ask in company with our fellow men not only how but also whether purpose and meaning can be discovered and expressed in people's lives today. The modern way of asking: "Where is thy God?" is no longer merely a theological and academic question but an observation based on the evidences of man's confusion and boredom, his emotional disturbance and mental disorder, his total lack of self-confidence and ability to orient himself in the contemporary world.

The challenge which the social sciences and psychotherapy present today to those Christian ministers who want to understand their people and themselves is no longer the debate of previous centuries which was concerned with whether the world evolved and developed under its own steam in accordance with physical and natural laws. Today the discussion has come one step further and one step closer to home, namely, to the self-appraisal of the human personality. Are we able to live in our world and organize our living together so that we can survive on human terms? In a highly impersonal, mechanized and demanding civilization, are the inner human resources both adequate and also sufficiently mobilized for the attainment of a creative common life?

The Christian ministry can no longer limit itself to proclamations about God and the world from which ethically correct behavior can be easily derived. Teaching and preaching at people on an exclusively rational level and about all that is outside of man is simply no longer sufficient. People no longer worry as much about what is outside of them as they do about what is inside of them. They want to find out whether they themselves are able to stand their ground against the impact from outside. They want to know how all their diverse and at times contradictory facets can be channeled into a total personality constructively interacting with the environment.

Since I believe strongly that the wide-spread current interest in the relationship between religion and mental health stems from the questions which are sketched above I have asked three theologians of different backgrounds and special interests to comment on the significance of the social sciences and psychotherapy for the relevance of the Christian ministry today. *Paul Tillich* was invited to open the discussion with his reflections on what kind of general theological outlook on the world is necessary in the attempt to make the ministry somewhat relevant again in our time. Many Christians and especially ministers have suspected for a long time that Tillich's appeal to such a multitude of people outside of the churches rests on his willingness to dim the challenge of the Christian faith and forsake its unique character. As editor I have dared to phrase Tillich's assignment in such a manner that he could not help but react to it and lay bare his basic appraisal of the uniqueness of the Christian faith and therefore the relevance of the ministry in our time. I am happy to report that Tillich has responded strongly and has come forward with a decided emphasis on the insight that the ministry must again find its proper place and distinct function precisely because otherwise it will lose its usefulness in our world. Between the twofold danger of either preserving the purity of the Christian faith by withdrawing from the challenge or adapting the Christian faith too easily and therefore losing its substance Tillich pleads for a rediscovery of the potency and relevance of the divine intention for man and his world. Such a rediscovery is to be hoped for only on the basis of a deeper and more radical understanding of the human predicament and a more concentrated effort to proclaim clearly the divine answer to the human quest for survival, meaning and forgiveness.

Reinhold Niebuhr broadens the theme. Focussing on the moral witness of the Christian faith he makes the important point that the whole tradition of Christian thought has throughout the centuries made an immense contribution to the quest for moral self-understanding and moral self-expression. He traces the highlights in the history of Christianity which make it clear how much the uniqueness of the human personality as a moral being has necessitated a deeper self-understanding as well as the awareness of being confronted by the sovereign Lord and sustainer of this world. Nevertheless, Niebuhr is quite willing to use the sharpened insights which some disciplines of modern culture offer in re-evaluating the findings and advice which Christian thinkers have given in the past. It certainly is and has to remain an open question whether in the light of modern knowledge in the social sciences and psychiatry we can merely take over the concepts and conclusions of our forefathers. In his own appraisal Reinhold Niebuhr gives us an instructive demonstration how Christian theology can benefit greatly from the challenge offered by the social sciences and psychotherapy in rendering the Christian faith still more relevant to the precise questions which modern man raises and for which he looks to the Christian minister for answers and guidance.

Samuel Miller goes one step further and suggests that the Christian church and its ministry have been deficient in their appreciation for the total human personality and not merely its rational and communal capabilities. Man is not merely an organism which thinks and therefore acts relatively wisely and according to his rational conclusions. People are also not merely gregarious animals who have to be brought together, entertained and playfully animated in the communal life of a congregation. The total domain of the instinctual and emotional not only demands recognition but represents the most fertile ground for those forces within the Christian tradition which work toward growth, maturity and vital expression of the total personality. The central challenge of modern psychotherapy for the Christian ministry is therefore to rediscover the full orbit of Christian symbols. Since Christianity speaks of the word which became flesh, it certainly comprises also those expressions of the instinctual and emotional which with the rational and moral embrace the totality of human experience and expression. It would be detrimental if the symbolic expression of profound life awareness were exorcised from the Christian life and practice and simply relegated to psychotherapeutic sessions, the arts, drama and literature. Symbols in their constantly changing power and expressions can make the Christian church and its ministers aware that human life is never as flat and black and white as rational theological concepts and words imply. The depth, mystery and fertility of religious experience and liturgical expression should refresh and reform the life of the church lest it become a petrifact of a once vital faith.

It is one thing to speak of the challenge which the Christian ministry and theological education face today from the social sciences and psychotherapy. It is another to proceed toward precise steps which allow the ministry to become relevant to the situation which the social sciences describe and psychotherapy deals with psychiatrically.

The psychiatrist, *Kenneth Appel*, has never given up his conviction that a personal faith is a decisive aspect of the human personality and therefore of its emotional and mental well-being. His practice has time and again brought him cases where the patient's religious commitment and outlook have played a very strong part either in his becoming sick or his maintaining, despite his sickness, at least some points of reference, some values which were not submerged by the mental distortions but which served as foci for rehabilitation. Furthermore, Dr. Appel believes that in very many cases in his own experience and in that of his colleagues a personal faith has helped some of the patients to a great measure to regain their sense of reality and outgrow their psychopathological predicament. Dr. Appel therefore points to an obvious need. It becomes imperative that ministers help their parishioners, whether or not they are emotionally disturbed and mentally sick, to become clearer in the awareness and actualization of their personal faith. The psychotherapist in turn has to become better acquainted with the genuine character and the substance of religious faith in order to appraise this facet of his patients' lives congenially and sympathetically. He will then be able to separate any psychopathological distortions of their religious outlook from the genuine and constructive religious forces that contribute to the healing process in psychotherapy.

In this chapter Dr. Appel does not expound a psychiatric theory or tell the reader all that he should know about modern psychotherapy. Rather, he concentrates on telling the minister how much he should know about psychiatry and how this knowledge should be integrated into his own pastoral work with parishioners and his cooperation with psychiatrists. As editor, I have urged Dr. Appel very strongly to focus on the kind of personality which a psychiatrist would consider mandatory in a pastor to facilitate possible collaboration between the pastor and the psychiatrist. Through all that Dr. Appel has to say to us it becomes evident that the response of the minister to the challenge of psychiatry must certainly not lie in a superficial acquaintance with psychiatric terms or an unskilled and therefore dangerous imitation of psychiatric methods. The clue to a truly helpful and relevant ministry lies in the pastor's own personality. A man who is rooted deeply in the reality of his own faith and who not only faces the difficulties of his existence and work but opens himself to the challenge from outside is ready to take the problems of his parishioners seriously. Only someone who has been deeply troubled by all those questions and problems which the parishioners may bring to him but has learned to bear them and look for a solution not in magic or a doctrinal dictum but in the process of constantly growing beyond that which he had known before into a new discovery of the reality of faith, will be in a position really to help his people. Psychiatry has revealed a depth of human suffering and confusion which heretofore we did not even think possible. The excitement of our response to the problem of being human in our time lies for the minister precisely in the surprising realization that however deep the abyss and darkness of human suffering and defeat may be, it is not the last word but rather the gateway toward the experience of a still deeper and certainly more realistic affirmation of life.

Starting from this experience the pastor will be able to recognize how much he can learn from the findings in the psychiatric profession and cooperate constructively with its representatives without ever losing the vision of his own pastoral work and the confidence in the unique contribution which his faith can make toward the maintenance and recovery of mental health.

Seward Hiltner has all this in mind when he asks what difference the impact of psychotherapeutic knowledge—in his personal case especially the work of Carl Rogers—makes in the attitude and proceedings of pastoral counseling. Can the minister still afford insensitively to assume that all of a person's problems boil down to a mere lack of good will or acquaintance with the teachings of the Bible? Hiltner proceeds to demonstrate on the basis of an actual case situation how a premature assertion of the pastor's own appraisal prevents the very therapeutic growth and struggle on the part of the counselee which might have issued in authentic faith and realistic action.

The willingness to sacrifice the traditional authoritarian and domineering attitude in pastoral counseling in order to learn with and from the counselee indeed requires of the minister a considerable degree of self-confidence and the courage to ask questions anew and critically re-evaluate what has been taken for granted heretofore. The reward consists in an ever new discovery of the reality of faith and its unexpected relevance to problems of human growth, failure and regeneration. The success of psychiatry has always originated in clinical honesty and willingness to learn. Psychotherapy thus challenges the pastoral counselor to test out whether such honesty and open-mindedness could not again unearth the most vital and relevant aspect of the Christian faith. The response of the pastoral counselor should not be to imitate psychiatrists in their own professional role. Far from it. Rather we should be stimulated to discover whether we could not be more effective and more satisfied in our pastoral work if we allowed the hidden ways of God in dealing with people to open for us new vistas on how the Christian faith demonstrates its own relevance.

Reuel Howe is dedicated to the education and the further training of those ministers who as pastors have given evidence of the capacity to play a vital role in accepting the challenge of modern times to the ministry and who respond by becoming men who live by their faith and radiate its relevance. He knows that as in any other profession they have the innate ability to learn in their own parish work from the experience of their successes and mistakes. But Howe is convinced that the initial theological education and training of prospective ministers should make them ready for such a learning experience in the parish ministry instead of misleading them into the notion that they learned in seminary all that there is to be learned and have merely to apply it in their own work according to the advice of their academic teachers. A minister can only respond to the challenge which he finds in his pastoral work if he has already been taught during his theological training to respond to the world as it is. This in turn means that theological educators should not confuse teaching with mere lecturing. It is an illusion to assume that the theological student is able to concentrate on the solely academic absorption of rational thought and concepts and then, digesting these on his own, become a minister who is able to use his knowledge of the Christian tradition as resource for his pastoral experience and for relevant actions.

Making the ministry relevant is not an exclusive task for the minister, but first for all those who are responsible for his education and training before he goes out into the ministry. Howe asks for a radical reorientation in theological education. He challenges the theological faculties to go beyond their traditional study and training programs. They are asked to include post-graduate studies for those ministers who have already been out in the parish and want time to reflect on their experience for the sake of still better and more relevant work in the future.

In the opening chapter, I have attempted to sharpen the common tenor in all the manifold contributions which the different writers have presented. I have therefore reformulated in more provocative terms the dispassionate observations of

the contributors in order to tempt the reader of this book out
of any observer seat he might occupy into an active participation in the common task of making the ministry relevant. Be
the reader a parishioner, minister, theological educator, social
scientist or psychiatrist, be he religiously committed and a member of a specific denomination or not, he cannot fail to see that
the future and the significance of American culture depends
at least partly upon whether the Judeo-Christian tradition
brings into play its significant vision of the place and function
of the human being in our world. We live in a time of decision
which requires that every religious and cultural institution
should demonstrate anew the right to the existence and survival
of their particular tradition. Those forces which have lost their
innate strength will vanish from the scene. The sooner we
recognize the kind of changes that are required of us the clearer
will be our vision of the future with respect to our particular
contribution. The shrinking of time and space on our earth has
brought to an end the era of self-contained isolationism of any
profession. We depend on each other.

A brief word may be in order describing the Harvard University Project on Religion and Mental Health out of which
this book has grown. A grant from the National Institute of
Mental Health has enabled Harvard University to experiment
in relating the insights of the social sciences and psychiatry to
theological education. The focus is on an understanding of the
human personality, on bringing together the religious doctrine
of man and the findings in the social sciences and psychiatry
rather than merely borrowing disconnected fragments of technical skill from these in pastoral counseling. Accordingly, and
in the light of teaching experience, the Project will, elsewhere,
offer curricular suggestions and textbook material to other
theological schools in the country.

                                        Hans Hofmann

CONTENTS

Outlook

HANS HOFMANN

HANS HOFMANN, native Swiss, came to this country after he had completed his graduate studies in Europe. He concentrated on systematic theology with special emphasis on the doctrine of man. Therefore, it was natural that he should have extended his academic and empirical interest into the areas of the philosophical, psychiatric, and social scientific concern with the human personality. After having written a systematic exposition of Reinhold Niebuhr he taught for four years at Princeton Theological Seminary. Since 1957 he has been the Director of the University Project on Religion and Mental Health and Associate Professor of Theology at Harvard Divinity School.

IN THE traditional organization of the theological disciplines, pastoral theology was designed to deal with the person of the minister and his concrete functioning within the parish life. This was always regarded as a rather simple assignment and therefore quite inferior to theoretical content courses, which explain the origin, development and nature of the Christian faith. The unchallenged assumption was that the essence of Christianity consisted of the absolute and by-God-revealed truth about God and man and their relationship in history, as it was recorded in the two testaments of the Bible, crystalized through the doctrines of the church and rationally understood through continuing theological reflection within the church. The doctrines of the church had merely to be taught and accepted, regardless of, and sometimes straight against, any rational doubts or worldly evidence to the contrary. On the basis of such an "absolute truth," man was expected to know right from wrong in the consideration of his life and predicament.

The role of the pastor was therefore to instruct his parishioners in the nature and implication of faith for their life conduct and to help them privately to come to the "right" personal decisions and to the vigorous implementation of these decisions in the life of the community. Small wonder that pastoral theology was regarded as rather an easy matter, since the personal and functional authority of the parson had only to be fully identical with the established authority of the revealed will of God, propagated by the self-confident teaching of the church.

The social atmosphere of the past was clearly favorable to such an understanding of the ministry. The morally trust-worthy individual, in discharging his public responsibility, was a crucial member of the community and its development. There was room, much room left for personal decisions on the part of the individual.

This situation was basically changed in the first half of the twentieth century. Technological skill, based on scientific dis-coveries, raised the standard of living in this country. The rapid growth of organized production interacted with a greater de-mand for goods. Meanwhile the goods lost their intrinsic value. The economic factor is demonstrably predominant in modern life, and more influential—in this country at least—than polit-ical, social or cultural factors. The human being has become the labor potential which, according to its usefulness, is put on the most suitable rung of the industrial ladder. Man's reward for his contribution to greater production is that he is able to consume more of what he produces. His prestige today is measured by his material possessions, which carry the sign of his success and achievement. The human being is hopelessly caught in the vicious circle of having to produce furiously in order to consume enough to keep up the living standard which is mandatory in his social class, and may eventually allow for his elevation to a higher social rank. In reality, though, his social goals are themselves carefully produced by another facet of production: the advertizing industry.

The tremendous change in the concept of the human factor in present-day economic development is best understood by looking at the educational revolution which is also taking place. The end of the nineteenth century saw the victoriously an-nounced liberation from a rigid educational structure. In pro-gressive education the child was meant freely to unfold his unique potentials of learning and understanding. On this basis everyone was seen as able to fulfill his individual promise and therefore contribute more successfully to the ever-growing human control over material, social and cultural circumstances. Today, this school of education is most bitterly criticized by those who are disappointed that such an approach has not allowed us to keep up with the striking scientific and technological progress achieved by other countries who have religiously adhered to the absolute superiority of scientific and technological advancement over the free development of the human personality.

But the human factor in our own economic development has been severely neglected precisely because people today are still under the illusion that a free society exists in this country. The previous rebellion against a puritan, victorian social sterility has turned into the far weaker, and probably futile attempt to understand and preserve independent human dignity in the giant industrial mill of production and consumption. The "man in the gray flannel suit" tries to escape his workaday business world by establishing—at considerable expense—a pleasurable privacy on the grounds of independent ownership. But the tyranny of professional demands closely dogs his homeward steps. Television punctuates its unprepossessing artistic presentations with skillfully suggestive advertizements of all those goods and facilities which he still needs in order to be happier and make his family happier. Illustrated catalogues and journals for home and garden tell him what equipment he will need to be up to date, to convert his comfortable home into a socially presentable place.

Man's frustration at being treated just as a labor potential is further increased by modern marketing, which diverts a genuine dissatisfaction with life into the desire for more and more goods. In the long run, this process is self-defeating because it inevitably leads to the breakdown of the very labor potential which the economy tries so carefully to preserve. There comes a moment when any man, regardless of his rank in the hierarchy of production, comes to the realization, even if it is a very dim one, that the mere thrill of still better and better production does not fulfill his human need for a deeper satisfaction; nor does the ever-mounting accumulation of goods and social privileges allow him to unfold his truly human potentials. But it would be wrong to think of this realization in very dramatic terms. The time has long since passed when we could pack our bags and escape civilization by "lighting out for the territory." This is no longer possible; we cannot leave civilization or the barrage of modern industry. Man today rebels in very meek and unadmitted terms. He begins to have headaches and ulcers, to have all kinds of physical diseases which do not account for themselves somatically. He has insomnia and nightmares, trouble with his wife, difficulties with his children and, in all, is no longer the friendly, vital fellow who was so well-liked because the world seemed so open to him. Indeed, it is no mistake to compare the subliminal, emotional crisis of modern man with the difficulties in adjustment which we know the menopause can bring to the female who has passed her reproductive function.

We are certainly not unaware of these difficulties in our time. The social sciences and human engineering have produced very impressive machinery of skilled investigation and effective statistical comparison by which they demonstrate the total ramification and implication of this acute human predicament. The facts are known and, by some, even understood. New disciplines of psychosomatic medicine and psychiatry cope with the physiological, emotional and mental aspects of our cultural disease. Psychoanalysis has developed an immensely subtle approach in peeling off the different layers of our confused reactions to life and our unadmitted defense mechanisms.

Moreover, it has related them to our previous inability to cope with our life-situation when we were still infants. Psychotherapy, which is most probably less helpful than we expect it to be, is still the most effective means known of laying bare our most crucial problems. It has now risen to a cultural significance which, in itself, is quite telling. It has produced objective, though not scientific, evidence that man, in his individual life, has always been and always will be dependent. The question only remains: what is he dependent on? Sigmund Freud, who took the philosophical ideas current at his time completely for granted, seems to have been convinced that the rational understanding of one's dependency allows for enough inner distance from it to make it tolerable. Carl Gustav Jung broadened this concept into the more sophisticated theory that man can tolerate himself and his life according to how well he understands himself and his intimate connection with culture throughout its past and present.

Most significantly, contemporary psychotherapy has joined ranks with another modern movement, existentialism. Their humanism is based on the individual and the individual alone, who is completely aware of and willing to accept the circumstances in which he lives. The three most striking aspects of the similarity between existentialism and psychotherapy are: the human ability to choose and decide—into which a person can throw himself and hence discover his true nature; the freedom to step courageously into the openness of interpersonal relationships, thereby revealing himself as he truly is, and encountering and accepting others on the same ground; finally, and most important, the recognition of the universe as primarily a human place to be constantly recreated in the light of man's understanding of himself.

The importance of such thoughts is easily recognized. It is no longer a question of the dichotomy between human subject and material object, abstract idealism and principles versus realistic materialism. The antagonism between transcendentalism and evolutionism no longer holds. It is man who sees himself as a unity, as a particle within the structure of the world, but with a very specific function: he is to discover not only what the world is all about and what it can be used for, but to bring to it the new and endlessly discovered dimension of meaning which breaks through his own self-understanding and therefore gives a human understanding to the purpose of the world. Man, who was the discoverer of the world, now becomes a discoverer of himself, with the very same ethos and methods with which he performed his former task. The underlying assumption is that the economic side of modern life, as we have described it above, has been permitted to become so tyrannical just because man has unconsciously lost his ability to assert himself as a human being. It is indeed astonishing to trace—in recent history—the naïveté which took the unique characteristics of the human personality for granted to such an extent that they were virtually powerless to contribute their proper function.

The decisive question about this new awareness and knowledge of the human factor will therefore be whether we use it to withdraw from participation in the mundane but crucial decisions about our future in order to introspect privately and irrelevantly upon ourselves; or whether we use it to accept the challenge which our modern economy offers us, namely to renounce the impotence of the human position in the mechanized organization of daily life and assume a human leadership in the ordering of society.

It is at this point that we have to discuss the place and function of the Christian ministry. It cannot be disputed that the Christian church at large often has accepted uncritically the economic development in this country. This is more than partly to be explained by the financial dependence of the church upon those who contribute the most and therefore also feel that they should

have most to say about the role of the church. The church, unfortunately, is no different from other institutions in its desire
to justify itself through external aggrandizement. Still more important, the church has sheepishly followed the withdrawal of
the human being from critical leadership in commerce and industry into a suburban escape where it can soothe its painful
loss of self-confidence. The sermons and the counseling sessions
of our contemporary pastors are full of petty trivialities which
have to be blown up into disproportionate problems because we
are neither willing to face our real problems, nor have we felt
the presence of any resources to deal with our profoundest predicament. The minister, lacking such resources, turns in his
bankruptcy to psychologically phrased sermons and psycholo-
gized counseling techniques. It is disastrous that the Christian
church should so enviously have borrowed—and without any
critical judgment—the psychiatric and psychological insights
and methods which, in themselves, are merely the result of our
inability to tackle our problems in the broader context in which
they have arisen. Because of their immoderate dependence on
psychiatry and psychology, the churches have been driven to
consider the individual instead of the community as a whole, the
latter being, in fact, their proper function. The human being,
therefore, finds nothing but his irreversible dependence, without
knowing what he can depend on in order to regain his dignity
and active forcefulness in dealing with his life situation.

There are those within the Christian church who believe the
remedy for this is the uncritical reaffirmation of an outdated outlook which may or may not have been the way our ancient forefathers once understood their faith and their functional place
in this world. It does not take much imagination to see the tremendously regressive mood in which, through the revival of
traditional pietism, the lost, confused and insecure man of
today is seduced into a futile identification with a world and a

world-view which, in retrospect, appears like a golden age, without any of the problems which we have to face today. It is no longer so easy to be told by the divines what life and the world are all about, from their origin to their final conclusion, and what, therefore, the precise right and wrong of any given situation really is.

It would be useless to criticize religious conservatism merely by replacing it with a more sophisticated and newly worded theological orthodoxy. The church is under the illusion that it is making progress, whereas in reality it is moving in a vicious circle. This illusion must be swept away; we must take the step of discovering the religious potentials of our own life-situation, independent of the religious tradition of the past. Once this is done, it would certainly be useful and enlightening to study the religious faith of past generations in order to understand the difference and similarity between their faith and ours. In this way we will bring to light the underlying meaning of faith in our time.

People have to become explorers again, adventurers as the six-teenth-century discoverer of a new continent, unbiased and unprejudiced like the modern scientist in his desire to be led by any dependable evidence that comes to him in his search. Our hypothesis is that religious orientation has given confidence and purpose to past generations. But everything that religion has said or meant in the past is only hypothetical, and must be tested in the laboratory of the contemporary individual's search for a lasting meaning for his personal life. This is why American con-gregations across the country could become one single research laboratory. For all too long, too many ministers have hampered the honest growth of their parishioners by misleading them into the belief that the Christian faith is one single, simple and ra-tional way of life, fabricated for them by their pastor into a neat parcel to be used in the dark hours when they are alone with their illusions and fears and want a narcotic to give them peace of mind. Some want to revive the concept of the pastor as the shepherd of his flock. It is hard to believe that modern people either want to or ought to follow their normally poorly educated minister without reservation. This only sanctifies a paralyzing status quo which is then sugarcoated with religious virtue to make it palatable. No individual can bear to take the responsibility of the ills of the world upon himself, nor should he be encouraged to do so. It is far better to enlist his positive struggle in throwing off these excessive and irrelevant burdens; only after this is accomplished is he free enough to accept life for what it is, and only then will he be able to participate effectively and to his own satisfaction in life.

When it is stated above that the religious activities among us should become a research ground for the discovery of the unique meaning of our lives, it is implied, of course, that there is no clear-cut meaning already given. On the contrary, it is the struggle for the discovery and verification of such a meaning that gives human life value and significance and, by this process, reveals what there is of worth in and for our time. The clergy are not primarily the religious caretakers, priests or teachers. They do not pretend to have the answer to the riddles of human life. Their task is to be critical and to sharpen the doubts of their parishioners on everything they have automatically accepted on the word of the church.

Most of us have grown weary by now of keeping our lives going without any real promise. But very few ask about the most vital element of life when they are not given guidance or the assurance that they are on the right track. What is meant here is the freedom to pause in the middle of all the pushing trivialities of our daily routine and ask questions about its basic significance and purpose. Should it deny us the fulfillment of our creative longing for the discovery of, and freshness in, our very human identity, which is, after all, the greatest treasure we possess? Let us be perfectly honest about this; there is no future for a free, human society if the push-pull rhythm of production for artificially stimulated needs is its highest authority. Human life-awareness begins with the elemental questions of "why" and "what for." The very asking of these questions is the breath of human dignity. In a society where no one dares to ask them, or where anyone who does is ostracized as an unproductive dreamer, it is clear that we have already succumbed to a total organization under remote control.

But what good does it do to ask a question to which there is no immediate answer? It must not be forgotten that the real drive for discovery, which has made science and technology so great in the immediate past, was always in the search for the unknown. Curiosity and not security is the clue to a better future. Even though there is no absolute answer, it is only the straightforward desire to find out those things which are not yet within the orbit of our manipulation that will further our progress. What gives us the confidence to explore the unknown?

At this point the hypothesis of the Christian faith meets the human situation. It states, arrogantly enough, that there is a creative force behind all life which may be conceived as personal and as God and which realizes itself through the very human beings who ask questions about the direction and purpose of their lives. It is said to be a self-revealing force, which does not float freely and unobtainably in the blue sky, nor does it rest forever untapped in the depths of the earth. Through the flesh and blood of average citizens, who have no claim to fame, and to whom Nietzsche referred as those "much too many," this force will break through into an organizing factor which will finally defy all the self-appointed military, political and business empires of this world.

The question therefore shifts from whether there is meaning

to life at all, to the embarrassing question of why meaning does
not realize itself through "my" existence. From philosophical
abstraction, the question turns into a personal and practical re-
appraisal of our own life conduct. Are our lives to be the mere
continuation of a traditional pattern, long since obsolete? Or are
we ready to forsake boredom and insignificance in order to em-
bark on the exploration of human potentials for our time? Both
psychotherapy and existentialism have forced this disturbing
question upon us. Both of them are born out of despair at the
incessant corrosion of human vitality by the useless trivialities
which dominate us in the midst of the breakdown of Western
culture with its old-fashioned philosophy, and obsolete social
and political concepts. But both psychotherapy and existentialism can only point out the destructive aspects of our previous life
conduct and outlook. Both can merely postulate that there is
more than this. Both are driven to expect it from within the human being and both have therefore largely settled for humanism.
It is simply to overtax average people like ourselves to expect
us to draw new impulse and meaning out of ourselves like a
phoenix which, miraculously enough, rises from its own ashes.
Man is not "for himself" and cannot find his freedom and satisfaction by assuming it. Here the Christian faith comes to the
most concrete formulation of its own hypothesis.

The force of life, of which we have spoken, is the force of
love, which powerfully enters the human life and takes man by
surprise, but so vehemently that he is compelled to abandon his
well-guarded self-protection and, in this way, becomes valuable
to others, who, in turn, can afford to respond. Certainly we
would be hopeless fools if we sacrificed ourselves for any principle, idea or doctrine, or even for the idolatrous image of an
anthropomorphic God. All of these are merely the expressions
of how people have experienced the force of love. Most certainly
life is always fore-given. But it is not our life until we take its

WINGATE COLLEGE LIBRARY
WINGATE, N. C.

mystery and promise more seriously and abandon the old ideas and illusions we may have had about it. Any religion which promotes an old-fashioned imagery and doctrinal concepts for their own sake is a disgrace, but Christianity, which does it directly contrary to the wish of its own founder who himself had to fight religious complacence, defensiveness and exclusiveness, is doubly disgraced.

Every single parishioner, in this sense, potentially re-creates the Christian faith in his search for and discovery of the meaning of life. The minister is the leader of this movement. He channels the forces against their own hopeless resignation in the face of a situation which seems too overpowering to be overcome. And it is precisely here that the hypothesis of the Christian faith can be supremely tested. This is the task of pastoral theology.

The ministry is made relevant where the pastor is relieved from standing for something which is not worth being stood for, unless it can prove itself again in the renewal of human freedom from its entanglement in trivialities. The minister is the researcher who reports his findings, failure and achievements to the centers of theological education. There, in turn, it will be the main task of theologians, starting with this alarming evidence, to reconsider, in its light, the total spectrum of the Christian tradition, including the Bible, the doctrines, church history and present-day church life. We constantly deplore that theological education generally does not attract the best college graduates, that those who enter upon theological education lose their independent curiosity and intellectual vitality, that neurotic disintegration and low motivation prevent our students from being mature or equipped to face the present-day challenge to Christianity. All this has one very good reason. We, the theological educators, ourselves lack the imagination to explore life on its own terms or even to compare the religious attitudes

of the past with contemporary Christianity. We ourselves do
not believe in the immediacy and effectiveness of our own faith
and therefore hide behind the ruins of our doctrinal systems,
liturgical customs and ecclesiastic offices. We do not have the
courage to be as empty-handed and unpretentious as our colleagues in science are and evidently can afford to be. We robe
ourselves in the assumed authority of God, and constantly confuse the innate human respect for the sovereignty of real life
with an idol that merely promotes our own theological presuppositions and religious bias.

Theological education must center in and be justified by a
pastoral theology which represents the challenge of contemporary life to religious tradition. Instead of turning ourselves into
irrelevant scholars of a faith which never pretended to be academic and which cannot survive such academic self-consciousness, we should enlist young men to join us in finding out where
that God, of whom we speak so all too frequently, is at work
today. If he is, as we say, sovereign and free, he will always take
us by surprise by being more human than we dare to be or expect
him to be.

We do not have to go very far to learn about the exact nature
of the human predicament. A multitude of studies on this subject confront us at this very moment. Indeed, if we were really
alive to their implication, we would take them seriously. The
era has long since passed when the sciences were hostile to any
inquiries which originated beyond their orbit. On the contrary,
the sciences welcome any means which would relate their ethos
to the more intangible aspects of human life. The fault of religion, as well as of idealistic humanism, has not been to be un-
scientific but to identify theoretical images with absolute truth.
It takes courage to admit that one does not have and will not
have any absolute answers, or to be willing to put the prelimi-

nary hypotheses to the test. Without this courage, the Christian ministry is doomed to disappear with the bourgeois culture that made room for it.

There is no trick or safe method to make the ministry relevant. The closer we come to the core of what being human means, the less we are prone to build neat, scientific or philosophical approximations. It is painful and frightening to look honestly at life as it really is. The greatest difficulty is to drop our conventional, often hypocritical, masks. We must do so if the Christian faith and its ministry is to be relevant in our time.

The Relevance of the Ministry in Our Time
and Its Theological Foundation

PAUL TILLICH

PAUL TILLICH came to this country after the Nazi regime had suspended him from his position as Professor of Philosophy of Religion at the University of Frankfurt. At Union Theological Seminary in New York he devoted many years of teaching to the areas of systematic theology and philosophy of religion. At the present time he is University Professor at Harvard and is writing the third and final volume of his *Systematic Theology*. He is well known far beyond academic circles for his attempt to correlate religion and culture, the existential question of human life and the divine answer as it is known in the Judeo-Christian tradition.

I

THE question I have been asked to discuss in this article is "what kind of general theological outlook on the world is necessary in the attempt to make the ministry somewhat relevant again in our time?" This indeed is an important, far-reaching and extremely difficult question. Let us first look at the assumptions implied in its formulation. Most obvious is the presupposition that the ministry is not relevant in our time. Not so obvious, but certainly present, is the presupposition that the ministry can be made relevant again for our time—at least "somewhat." This "somewhat" expresses a profound skepticism about the possibility of making the ministry again as relevant as, according to its own claim, it should be. Further, the question as formulated presupposes the belief that a special type of theology could be found which would make the ministry more relevant or, at least, would contribute to such relevance.

Let me first state at the outset that I accept these assumptions, though with some qualifications. As bearers of the Christian message, ministers can never become completely irrelevant. If this were not so, the question of how to make it again relevant would be of small importance, actually of not more importance, for instance, than the question of how a vanishing fashion could be made relevant again—in the interest of some manufacturers. (In our case, the manufacturers would be replaced by the ministers.) Therefore, a serious treatment of the question of the relevance of the ministry presupposes that the ministry, in rep-

resenting the Christian message, stands for something of ultimate significance, something which is independent of any change
of fashion in thought and life. It is my conviction that this is the
case, and only on this basis can I take seriously the question put
to me as one worthy to be dealt with.

There is another qualification I must state: It is not true (and
certainly not meant to be true) that the ministry has become
totally irrelevant to our time. There are many people who not
only "go to church" regularly, but who are made aware of the
existential significance of the devotional acts through the guidance of their minister and his interpretation of the Christian
message. Even the typical suburbanite who attends Sunday services is not only and not always a representative of suburban con-
formity. He is sometimes grasped and transformed by what he
experiences in a particular service. Even a minister who is a poor
preacher can make his message relevant for some people through
the liturgy and through his "being."

After stating these two qualifications referring to the relevance of the ministry in our time, I can express my agreement
with the skeptical self-restriction in the form of the question
(the "somewhat") and also with the assumption that theology
can contribute to a definite increase in the relevance of the
ministry.

If these qualifications are accepted, one may ask what contributions can theology make to increase the relevance of the ministry? In order to answer this question, one must first elaborate
the factors which have made the ministry largely irrelevant for
our time.

Something can be irrelevant for something else for two reasons. It can be irrelevant because it is not understood in its
relevance, and it can be irrelevant because it has no essential
relation to that for which it claims relevance. It is for the second
reason that many people believe that the ministry is irrelevant

for them and for our time generally. According to them the
ministry has nothing to give which has essential significance
for man. If one believes, however, that the Christian ministry
can be made relevant again, one must reject this view and accept the first alternative—that it is irrelevant because it is not
understood in its relevance. It is this problem which shall concern us here.

The Christian ministry has ceased to be understood in its
relevance not only by those outside but also by those inside
the churches. The former deny any relevance of the ministry,
the latter see it in the wrong place. But both those outside and
those inside are dependent on the cultural development which
has transformed the image of the Christian ministry fundamentally. In making this statement I speak as a Protestant, well
aware of the fact that the situation in the Catholic Church is
different because Rome has resisted the lay principle which
appeared simultaneously in the Renaissance and the Reformation, and which today dominates secularism as well as Protestantism. Certainly, there are individual Roman Catholics who
feel the problem for themselves, but who would hardly make
a theological issue out of it. The problem we have to deal with,
therefore, is the problem of the relevance of the Christian
ministry for the secular world and for Protestantism insofar as
it has been transformed by the secular world.

For it is not Protestantism as such which has made the
Christian ministry irrelevant. The principle of the priesthood
of all believers has removed the hierarchical position of the
ministry. It has removed priesthood as a special, sacramentally
consecrated degree, but it has not removed the function of the
minister. On the contrary, it has given to the minister the highest
function that Protestantism knows, namely, to preach the
"Word," which includes the administration of the sacraments
and (in Calvinism) the exercise of the discipline. Certainly, in

Protestantism every Christian layman can perform these activities in principle (though not in the regular life of the Church). But as soon as a layman does so he acts as a minister, and the problem of the relevance of the ministry refers to him as much as to the formally called minister. Relevance is especially important for the counseling function of the minister (preaching applied to the individual situation).

Every Christian (including the psychotherapist) can become a priest for another Christian. It is not the professional task of the psychotherapist to become a minister. But it is possible that through his activities as physician and through his personality, priestly help is given to his patient. If this happens, the problem of the relevance of the Christian ministry refers to him as to any ordained minister. He only should not confuse his professional with his "priestly" help.

If we assume the rightful claim of the ministry to be that the minister pronounces, preaches, teaches and in counseling mediates the "Word of God," no question can arise about the relevance of his ministry for every human being. For "Word of God" means the self-manifestation of that which concerns everyone ultimately. And, certainly, nothing could be more relevant for man than what concerns him ultimately. If then, in spite of this assumption the function of the ministry has become irrelevant, this only can mean that the majority of ministers do not preach and teach the "Word of God" in such a way that it can be understood and received as a matter of ultimate concern by the people of our time. And this is the thesis to which our considerations finally come down: The ministry has lost its relevance insofar as it cannot communicate the Christian message, which *is* a matter of ultimate concern, *as* a matter of ultimate concern—religiously speaking—as the "Word of God."

The cause of this situation is not that the ministry of our

time is worse, spiritually (or Spiritually—according to its human spiritual or its divine Spiritual power), than any other ministry in the history of the Church. On the contrary, I would insist that it is better and in some respects far superior to several other ministries of the past. In spite of this, it has lost its relevance for a large number of people in the midst of our present Christian civilization.

The reason for the irrelevance of the Christian ministry in our time is that it has not learned to speak to the people of a largely secularized world in such a way that they feel: this message concerns us ultimately; it is a matter of "to be or not to be" for us. This is the case in spite of the fact that there are many highly educated, theologically learned, socially aware, morally committed and religiously devoted persons within the ministry. But together with the less outstanding members of their group, they suffer from serious and almost insoluable conflicts which are produced by their encounter with a secularized world, outside and inside the churches.

II

There are forms of what I would call the "pseudo-relevance" of the ministry. The word does not mean that the functions falling under this judgment are irrelevant; but it does mean that they are not able to make the ministry relevant as ministry. This refers to the social, the political, the educational, the psychotherapeutic activities of ministers. They all are relevant for human life. But none of them represents the meaning of the ministry as ministry. None of them makes the minister relevant as minister. It is not unimportant that there are groups (congregations) who, under the directions given by a minister, provide some kind of community for people who would otherwise remain lonely. It is not unimportant that the congregations provide occasions where people can eat together, play together, discuss and dance together in an atmosphere which stands under the judgment of Christian principles. But from the point of view of the meaning of the ministry, all this is pseudo-relevant. It has the tendency to cover up the basis for the minister's claim to be relevant. It makes him into a director of social activities in a service club, and it often prevents him from concentrating on the function which should make him relevant—that of pronouncing and repeating the message of a new reality.

Another form of pseudo-relevance of the ministry is its development into a political agency alongside other organizations. Again, we must say that it is of great importance that the voice of the Church be heard in public affairs. It is certainly one of the shortcomings of the Continental-European churches that this responsibility was and is still neglected. But if the Church addresses itself to matters of the political organization of men and mankind, it must do so as the Church. The relevance of the ministry lies not in its political utterances, nor in their possible value, but in its representation of the source from which such utterances should come. If churches work as political pressure groups under the leadership of their ministers, they do what other groups also do, while no other group can replace the Church. Only by embodying and preaching the new reality on which it is based can the Church and its ministry be relevant for our time.

Even the educational activities of the ministry do not make it relevant as ministry. A minister may become a well-known educator such as college president or leader in an educational association, but this does not make him relevant as a member of the ministry. It makes him important through his professional qualities which have developed partly (under the impact of his ministerial background. But the relevance of the ministry as such is not determined by the presence of such qualities in a minister. As a minister he represents the new reality from which educational consequences may be felt, by himself or by others. This even refers to the teaching of religion. Such teaching may be a contribution to the general educational process in which all subject-matter should attain some relevance for the pupil. But if the minister achieves no more than this he could be replaced by any other qualified teacher of religion. Only if his teaching has the character of inducing members of the younger (or sometimes older generation) into the reality of Christian existence does he act relevantly as a minister.

All this refers also to the new, extremely significant relation of the ministry to psychiatry and the many facets of psychological help. It can be of great advantage for mentally disturbed or diseased patients if the minister collaborates with the psychotherapist toward their recovery. And at least in some respects, the theologically and psychologically educated minister often sees more than the psychotherapist alone. But even if this were the case to a higher degree than it actually is, it would not make the minister relevant as a minister. Only if his awareness of the psychological problems in ministerial counseling ("care of souls") helps him to exercise this activity better is it a factor in the relevance of the ministry as ministry. For as a minister he tries to communicate the healing power of the Christian message which is the power of reconciliation of the estranged and reunion of the separated. The relevance of the Christian ministry will be decreased if, along with their functions as club directors, pressure-group agents and educators, many of our younger ministers also consider themselves as dilettante psychoanalysts. There is no doubt that this is a danger today.

III

The Christian ministry is relevant to our time insofar as it is able to communicate the message of the new reality as an answer to the questions implied in human existence. This, however, is a task of almost insuperable difficulty, and it would be impossible if it were dependent on the good will of the ministers and theologians alone. But this is not the case. History shuts and opens doors. It is history which has created the problem of the irrelevance of the minister and not the inevitable deficiencies and failures of ministers, theologians and Church authorities. And it is history which gives the churches opportunities to restore the relevance of the ministry. But in order to take advantage of these opportunities, theologians and ministers must become aware of them and must find the courage to use them. This is not impossible, and the Church has survived many periods of near-irrelevance because at least a few of its members have understood the situation and were driven by the Spiritual power of the Christian message to react to the situation creatively.

It was the development of an independent secular culture in the Western world which pushed the ministry into a corner of the social fabric. In the view of industrial society (which is the destined structure of Europe and America, and increasingly of all nations throughout the earth) the Christian message is a strange body of forms of life and thought. One can show this from many sides of the total structure of our culture, and it has been described in many successful attempts to analyze our situation in sociological, psychological and philosophical terms. In all of them one thing is manifest. Modern secularist culture is concentrated on the inquiry into and handling of objects and their relation within the encountered universe. It does not transcend the calculable and manageable world, but thinks and lives inside its boundaries. The emphasis may be more on nature and its technical transformation or on man and the development of his potentialities, more naturalistic or more humanistic. In any case the boundary line of the totality of finite objects is carefully kept and not transcended in any direction. In a metaphorical language one could say the "dimension of depth and height" is sacrificed to the horizontal dimension. One does not look downwards or upwards, but one looks ahead and one goes ahead in all directions.

But the Christian message comes out of the vertical dimension and tries to turn mankind into the direction of depth and height. Wherever it is heard it shakes the universe of finite objects. But it is not heard, because man, determined by the world as it is seen and shaped in industrial society, shuts himself off to any attack from the vertical dimension, the dimension of the ultimate in meaning and being.

This is not always done by a plain rejection of the Christian message or of religion generally, indeed, it is comparatively seldom done in this way (Baron d'Holbach in the 18th, Nietzsche in the 19th, Russell in the 20th century). Usually it is done by methods which make the Christian message irrelevant. Christianity is tolerated either as an emotional outlet, or it is used as an ornament pasted on the all-too-sober building of our daily life. And there are the more refined forms of using it, mentioned already in the description of the pseudo-relevance of the ministry. In contrast to these indirect ways in which industrial society makes the message of the ministry irrelevant, a direct rejection gives it at least a negative relevance and makes the turn to a positive relevance easier.

IV

The next question, however, is: How does the Church itself react to the secular culture which has pushed it into irrelevance? It has used two ways to remain relevant, both of which must be considered as failures: A radical rejection of and a radical adaptation to secular culture. One could follow this through, both with respect to the life and to the thought of the Church. It is the latter problem which concerns us here, the message which the ministry tries to communicate to the people of our time. It is the relevance of the thought of the Church which we have to discuss. The choice of alternative, preservation or adaptation, has been the great problem ever since the rise of industrial society and its secular forms of thought.

Preservation is mainly represented by what is called orthodoxy in Europe and fundamentalism in this country, adaptation by what is called theological humanism or liberal theology on both continents. Both approaches are partly responsible for the irrelevance of the ministry today. The way of preservation makes the Christian message unapproachable, the way of adaptation makes it superfluous. To make it both approachable and meaningful another course must be found. A person who is grasped by the Christian message is necessarily convinced that the power of the Christian message itself will cut such a way through the jungle of contemporary confusions and distortions of this message, one which avoids the shortcomings of the other two. He assumes that if Jesus as the Christ is rightly called the "Logos," i.e., the principle of the divine self-manifestation, there can be no time in past and future when the Christian message is irrelevant. On the basis of this conviction, I shall give some examples characterizing the third way, which is neither preservation nor adaptation.

V

Man's power of transcending the given endlessly in all directions does not remove his finitude, although this power is often used in order to cover up the nakedness of his finitude. Man's finitude is experienced as the anticipation of one's own death, as the insecurity and the ever-present threat of suffering, as the restlessness of the internal as well as the external life, as the lone-

liness in the midst of crowds and friends, as the anxiety of non-
being and being. When the minister quotes the first words of the
Apostolic Creed: "I believe in God the Almighty, maker of
heaven and earth," he should relate them to the predicament of
human finitude if he wants these words to become relevant to
his congregations. He should not give the impression that he
told the story of a far-removed past when an all-powerful being
suddenly decided to use his creative powers, but he should point
to the questions in the hearts and minds of the listeners to which
those words imply an answer. The creaturely situation of everything in time and space is acknowledged and accepted, but
every creature is seen as rooted in a creative ground from
which it comes and to which it goes and by which it is sustained
and directed in its life-span. The certainty of this assertion
and the courage to maintain it by taking the inescapable
doubt into itself is the courage out of which the words of
the Creed once were born. They are expressions of the
courage of faith and not doctrines to be believed on authority. They point to the eternal, wherein one can find the
power to bear the natural anxiety of having to die. These
words of the Creed show an all-embracing Presence which trans-
forms creaturely loneliness into solitude, though in contact with
the eternal and with the power of universal communion. They
pronounce a rest which does not remove but which transcends
the restlessness of the heart. They answer the question of suffering and the riddle of inequality, not by explaining it in moral or
educational terms, but by showing a possible answer in an eternal destiny for every creature. Such a message was and is and
will be relevant, so long as men are men; but it is a message which
must be liberated from the doctrinal and ritual dust which has
fallen upon it and has made it unapproachable for ministers and
congregations alike.

VI

Whether in creeds or in hymns or in prayers, Christianity is centered around the being of Jesus as the Christ. Innumerable times the minister uses the words Jesus Christ, emphasizing either the Christ-element in the name—according to the method of preservation against the secular world—or the Jesus-element in the name—according to the method of adaptation to the secular world. In both cases he fails to make the words Jesus Christ relevant to his partly or fully secularized listeners. "Christ" means for most of them a half-divine being, coming from a heavenly place, appearing on earth as the man Jesus of Nazareth, performing the work of atonement, returning to the place from which he came. This myth is so strange to them that they not only reject its literal interpretation, but also its symbolic power, if it is "deliteralized." Is there a way of making the combination of the name "Jesus of Nazareth" with the old symbol of the "anointed one" (the Messiah or Christ) meaningful and relevant to the secularized state of mind of our society? It is certainly not possible if one removes the Christ-element and tries to retain the Jesus-element by emphasizing the humanity of Jesus. For Jesus as simply a prophet or martyr is not the foundation on which church and ministry are built; his "teachings" alone do not constitute the message of the reconciliation of an estranged world and of a "new reality" under the conditions of existence.

But this is just what is asked for by the man of today. He is not only aware of his finitude, but also of his guilt and the estrangement from his true being. Under the cover of secular humanism there is a layer of torturing uneasiness about a life which in spite of its high moral standing is far-removed from fulfilled humanity. Guilt-feelings in many forms, genuine and neurotic, appear in psychotherapy and counseling in most unexpected places. It raises the question which lies at the center of the Christian message: How is it possible to conquer the inner conflict between the good that one wills and the bad that one does?

The minister should not try to answer this question by removing its seriousness. He probably would not do it in the way many psychoanalysts have done, by blurring the difference between genuine and neurotic guilt or deriving all guilt feelings from neurotic disturbances. But the minister often does what no psychoanalyst would do—he may reply to the confession of guilt with moral commands. Such a reaction makes the minister less relevant to the men of our time than the psychotherapist, and consequently, they flee to him away from the ministry. The Christian ministry is one of reconciliation. And it is a sad fact that many people can find the word of reconciliation, not in the words of the minister, but in the words of the psychological helper. Moralistic preaching does not aid people in the situation of despair about themselves; it drives them into deeper despair or into a compromise between their actual being and what they feel they ought to be. The minister as a mere representative of the moral law has pseudo-relevance, but he lacks the relevance of one who has the message of reconciliation.

But after this has been accepted, everything depends on the way this message is given. Here irrelevance can follow from a method of preservation in which the symbols of atonement (the Cross and the Resurrection of the Christ) are communicated in language to which the secularized mind has no approach whatsoever. The traditional liturgical language is especially extensive in this respect, condemning to irrelevance the minister who has to use it.

It is possible for man today to understand a description of the human situation in honest terms of guilt and despair or an analysis of "man against himself" (without using terms like "original sin"), and the quest for a power of healing is deeply rooted even in people who call themselves naturalists or humanists.

A message which describes this situation, using in its description both the Biblical and the immense cultural material is certainly relevant for our time; it formulates the question implied in the situation of "man against himself"; and it can formulate it more adequately than the secular mind because it does so in view of the answer given as the center of the Christian message, the word of reconciliation. The form of this answer, however, is equally influenced by the form of the question. It points to the appearance of Jesus as the Christ as the decisive manifestation of a new reality, that of reconciliation and healing. Such an interpretation of the figure of Jesus as the Christ is adequate to a secular world in which the mythological symbolism of classical theology has no possible appeal. The picture of the "Suffering Servant" in both Old and New Testaments is able to grasp the human mind in every sociological and psychological situation. It transcends all theological interpretations, it gives an element of truth to all of them, it is open to new interpretations, and makes the ministry relevant wherever it is pronounced. It conquers the anxiety of guilt in many who do not know any theological explanation of this fact. The relevance of the ministry lies not in a theology of the Cross, but in the vision of the Crucified.

The hardest task of the ministry is to make the Christological symbolism relevant to the people of our time. There are many who turn away from Christianity to mystical types of piety, e.g., Medieval, Buddhist, Hindu or Taoist mysticism, because this enables them to experience the "vertical" dimension without being bound to doctrinally formulated symbols which receive their material from concrete historical events and express the life of a particular historical community. If the minister is

not able to show the universally human significance of the
Christian message in its particularity he remains irrelevant for
our time. (It should be remembered that classical theology,
especially in the first centuries of the Church, was fully aware
of this problem and tried to solve it with the Logos doctrine.)

VII

The most conspicuous expression of our contemporary situation is not the quest for the conquest of finitude or guilt, but for
the conquest of meaninglessness. This is an immediate consequence of secularism in the stage of emptiness. It is this situation
which puts the ministry to its main test; here the decision is being
made about its relevance or irrelevance for our time. But here
history also has provided support by making the most sensitive
minds of our time aware of the predicament of present society.
Existentialist art, literature and philosophy are witness to it. A
ministry which remains a stranger to such witness condemns
itself to irrelevance; a ministry which uses these expressions of
our predicament and shows their relation to the Biblical literature and the Christian message can become immensely relevant
to our time.

When the minister speaks of the divine Spirit (not only in the
liturgy or once a year in a sermon at Pentecost) he should relate
this term to the personality problems as they are discussed in
Existentialism and analytic psychology. He should remove the
"ghostly" connotations of terms like "Holy Ghost" or "Holy
Spirit" and should show that in these symbols the answer is contained to the questions raised abundantly and profoundly in our
time. They represent the dimension of depth in man's spiritual
life—religiously speaking: God manifesting his presence in the
center of man's personal being. But such an answer can be relevant only if it is united with the insights into the dynamics of
man's life as a personality, generally and individually. Formulas

like the guidance, power, love, communion of the Divine Spirit are irrelevant if their significance for the relation of the unconscious and the conscious in man is not taken into consideration, or if the structures of moral and conventional repression are not understood, or if the demonic-divine ambiguity of "being religious" is not described, or if the self-contempt and self-hate in what is called "self-love" is not recognized, and the immensely difficult act of necessary self-love in the sense of self-acceptance is not emphasized. A minister who is not aware of these problems and speaks emphatically (at Pentecost) about the gift of the Holy Spirit is irrelevant to our time.

The last example I want to use is the symbol "Kingdom of God" in its historical and transhistorical implications. The ministry cannot become relevant to our time if it identifies the Kingdom of God—as it often did in the last half-century—with the results of man's scientific, technical, political and educational progress. Whatever the character of this progress is, to call it the actualization of the Kingdom of God is more than wrong; it is superfluous. The religious glorification of progress by a theology of adaptation has proved to be disastrous for the relevance of the ministry. But a return to the separation of the idea of the Kingdom of God from history would make the idea equally irrelevant for our time. It would leave history to itself without the dimension of the Eternal in it. Such a "transcendentalism" would remove the dynamic, fighting, anti-demonic, inner-historical character of the Kingdom of God and transform it into a static heaven into which the individual soul desires to enter. The question of the meaning of history and its relation to the eternal would remain unanswered; the symbol "Kingdom of God" would be irrelevant to man's historical existence. And, consequently, it would be irrelevant to a period of history in which the question of our historical existence is predominant. To speak about the "Kingdom of God," the nearness of which is, after all, the basic message of the New Testament, without referring to the question of the aim of history, the tragic ambiguity of all historical events, the powers, chances and forces of history, the relation of the individual to history, makes the ministerial function of pronouncing the coming of the Kingdom of God irrelevant.

For large groups in our time—even within the churches— the function of the ministry is to assure and reassure the continuation of temporal life after death. Since this belief is also one shared by many secularists, propagated by many moral, political and even economic interests, the role of the ministry in supporting this propaganda would constitute another form of pseudo-relevance. But the situation is more serious. The function of the ministry with respect to the popular belief in the immortality of the soul is to reject it and to replace it by the faith in eternal life above the temporal process. At this point relevance would mean basic and courageous criticism of ego-centered popular superstition; but it would also mean an answer to the question of finitude, the inequality of individual destiny, the meaning of life and the aim of history. Each of these questions is relevant at all times, including our own time. A ministry, able to speak to these problems and to live on the basis of the answers that it has the Spiritual power to give would be more relevant to our time than any other group. To point with inner authority to the eternal is the most relevant function men can perform today.

The Christian Moral Witness and Some Disciplines of Modern Culture

REINHOLD NIEBUHR

Reinhold Niebuhr was Charles A. Briggs Graduate Professor of Ethics and Theology and Vice-President of Union Theological Seminary in New York. A highly creative parish experience in Detroit stimulated a life-long interest in the social, economic and political forces which converge to create our present situation. He found in the deepest strata of the Christian tradition insights which could be used both as tools and vision for grappling with the contemporary crisis. Author of many books, he has presented his thought most systematically in his *The Nature and Destiny of Man*.

Our Christian faith is grounded in the conviction that in Christ we have the "wisdom and the power of God," that is to say the final key for the understanding of life and for its fulfillment. But it is a sorry witness to the truth in Christ to treat the gospel as a kind of panacea for all the ills of human life and history, which will be efficacious if it is only believed with fervor. Such an interpretation reduces the Christian faith to magic. On the contrary, we must approach the problems of the Christian ministry and the witness to the truth of the gospel in terms of the scriptural precept "By their fruits shall ye know them." The only way of validating the Christian faith is to prove it a resource for overcoming the perils of both death and sin; and for relating ourselves to our neighbors creatively, thus fulfilling the law of love.

To overcome the perils of death and sin means to come to grips with the incongruity of human existence, with the fact that man is so great and so small, or in Pascal's phrase "Such a monster, a prodigy, a worm." He shares the brevity of life with all mortal creatures; but he is the one creature who knows that he will die, and is therefore anxious with the fear of death. His "sin" is that he tries to avoid or obscure this human predicament by various forms of self-worship, grasping after security, power and wealth and claiming to have a greater degree of wisdom and virtue than mortal creatures can have. The evils which arise perpetually in human history are due, not so much to "sloth" or the failure to fulfill human potentialities, but to what the Greek dramatists called *hybris* and Augustine translated as *superbia* or pride. Human freedom can be destructive as well as creative, in short, because human beings refuse to accept the limited character of our creaturely finiteness and use their freedom for the sake of hiding their finiteness. Basically Pascal is right, that we find "only in the simplicity of the Gospel, an answer for both the dignity and the misery of man." The weakness of all or most rational philosophies is that they can't digest the incongruity of human existence; and, to quote Pascal again, "They tell man of his dignity and tempt him to pride or of his misery and tempt him to despair." Whether Pascal was right in his analysis of the inadequacies of the philosophies, we are committed to the Christian faith as a key to the understanding of the human situation. But an affirmation of this faith does not produce lives which validate it. The faith must be validated in the church by a ministry which helps men to find themselves and know themselves in an increasingly complicated culture; and to establish some viable human community in an increasingly complex technical civilization. Obviously this cannot be done if the Christian ministry does not maintain creative contact with all the disciplines of culture. Fortunately, the temptation of European continental Protestantism, expressed in Barthian thought, to guard the truth of the Christian faith by destroying all contacts with the disciplines of culture, is not our temptation, though we may suffer from a contrasting temptation, of losing the unique and distinctive sources of vitality by a too subservient attitude toward the modern disciplines. "Liberal Protestantism" was, after all, the product of the effort of the Christian church to come to terms with the outlook of the Enlightenment, which ended rather catastrophically by the abdication of the Christian tradition to the characteristic illusions of the Enlightenment about both human nature and human history.

But this failure of Liberal Protestantism must not persuade the church as the bearer of the Christian faith to bury its treasure

for the sake of preserving its purity. A new effort must be made
to relate every truth and insight in any discipline of culture to
the Christian interpretation of life, in order that we might be
as helpful as possible to modern man, as he faces the perils of
our contemporary culture and the greater perils to the integrity
of spirit and to genuine community in a modern technical civilization.

Such an effort must appropriate whatever insights are available and valuable in the disciplines of culture and must reject
those aspects of those disciplines, which either detract from the
"dignity" of man by trying to fit him into a naturalistic frame of
thought, thus denying his uniqueness, or which obscure his "misery" by obscuring the paradox that man's creative and destructive possibilities stem from the same source, which is his freedom over nature.

We must analyse this task of a creative relation of our faith to
our culture by distinguishing the disciplines, which might enrich the understanding of the human self as individual, more particularly the psychological disciplines and more specifically
those which are indebted to depth psychology; and the social
sciences and historical and political disciplines which may throw
some light on the problems of the human community. The second effort must be made in the light of a modest appreciation of
the fact that it is not possible to fulfill the commandment "Thou
shalt love thy neighbor as thyself" without understanding all the
patterns, laws and recurrences of the structure of the human
community as it has existed through the ages and as it has developed in a technical age.

In analysing the relation of theological instruction to psychiatric disciplines, it is well to recall that many seminaries already possess chairs which may be entitled "Religion and Psychiatry" or which may bear the traditional title of "Pastoral
Theology" but which, in any case, seek to make available some

degree of knowledge drawn from psychiatric disciplines for the purpose of making pastoral counseling wiser and more fruitful. Naturally these efforts in the realm of practical theology have hitherto been limited to the aspects of the human psyche where there is no clear dividing line between neurotic anxiety, which must be dealt with clinically, and "existential" anxiety which may be defined as the basic anxiety of human existence, a concomitant of human freedom and finiteness. The difference between neurotic and existential anxiety spells the difference between the ills which must be dealt with clinically and the basic religious problems with which a religious counselor can and must deal.

The general theory underlying courses in psychiatry in theological institutions is that they cannot and should not prepare the counselor to deal clinically with neurotic problems, but to know enough about the symptoms of neuroses to refer prospective patients to proper psychiatric specialists. I do not challenge this theory and I believe that this is still the limited function of courses in religion and psychiatry. But I also see the possibility of enlarged courses doing much more than preparing religious counselors to discern the border and border-line cases. They might have the purpose of exploring the endless complexities of the relation of love to self-love in the human self; of the creative and destructive possibilities of human freedom.

There is no reason to amend or change anything in the basic paradox in which Jesus himself puts the relation of self-love to love. That paradox is contained in the simple statement "Whosoever seeketh to gain his life will lose it and whosoever loses his life for my sake and the gospel will find it." We could translate this paradox as follows: Self-seeking is, if consistently followed, destructive. The self is too large and too small for its greatness to be contained in its smallness. The self cannot be itself within itself. It must fulfill itself beyond itself. Therefore, any consistent self-seeking means self-destruction. But, on the other hand, the Christian faith does not deny the legitimacy of self-realization. In this it is distinguished from both Buddhism and all forms of Christian mysticism, which seek the elimination of selfhood.

The paradox states the attitude of the Christian faith toward the problem of love and self-realization succinctly and accurately. Self-realization is recognized as not only legitimate but desirable. But it cannot be the intended end of action. It can only be the by-product of self-giving. Augustine probably came closer to approximating the classical paradox in his teachings on love and self-love than any other theologian in his distinction between two forms of *amor sui* or self-love. The self which loves itself simply, declared Augustine, destroys itself; but the self which loves itself in God, truly loves itself. Even this Augustinian formula is faulty, because his Neo-Platonic orientation prompted him to find no place for the love of the neighbor and to express the idea that the self must find itself in terms of the self's love of God.

Kierkegaard tries to solve the problem by suggesting that Jesus did not rule out self-love in the well-known love commandment "Thou shalt love thy neighbor as thyself." The "as thyself," according to Kierkegaard, merely sets the norm. Jesus was saying in effect: "You want to know how much you ought to love thy neighbor? Your love of him ought to be equal to the degree of your self-love." The trouble with this solution is that it does not exhaust the wisdom of the paradox about self-realization and self-giving.

Even with these defects, the theories of Augustine and Kierkegaard are superior to many theories both of Catholicism and Protestantism. Catholic asceticism not only assumes that self-regard is unambiguously evil but that it can be suppressed by strenuous effort. Martin Luther's strenuous anti-asceticism was due to his conviction, derived from his experience as a monk, that self-regard could not be suppressed out of a sense of duty. But he thought it might be overcome by grace. The question is whether Luther's idea of *agape* in the state of grace was not too perfectionist, despite his well known *justus et peccator simul*, that is his insistence that man redeemed, remained a sinner. Despite this insistence he certainly pictured the love of the "redeemed" man in too perfectionist terms. No one can be quite as un-self-regarding as Luther suggests in his description of the motives of the man who has been set free of self-regard by the assurance of divine forgiveness.

If Luther was mistaken in his estimate, certainly the whole of nineteenth century Protestant liberalism, including the social gospel school, was mistaken in regarding self-giving as a simple moral possibility. Practically no school of Christian thought fully explained the endless complexities and varieties of the combination of self-regard and love in all stages of human perfection and imperfection. These complexities, illuminating the endless varieties of self-giving and self-realization, may be said to represent the unsolved problem of the Christian understanding of the self's moral and religious problem, or the understanding of the self in the twin dimensions of its dignity and its misery.

A superficial view of the possible contribution of depth psychology toward the solution of this problem may lead to pessimistic conclusions. What possible contribution can be expected of either Freudian pessimism or Neo-Freudian optimism to this problem, one might well ask?

Yet it is a fact that despite the obvious defects of both Freudian and Neo-Freudian thought, modern psychiatry has evolved insights about the relation of persistent self-regard to human creativity, which may enrich the Christian understanding of man tremendously. Freud is commonly credited for giving a scientific and naturalistic version of the Christian doctrine of original sin. It is true that Freudian pessimism is the closest approximation of Christian realism in the context of modern naturalism. But the defects in this pessimism are obvious. There is no real apprehension in the thought of Freud of the true dimension of the self-transcendent self. The freedom of the self to judge itself is obscured by the concept of the "super-ego," which is nothing more than the internalization of the community's pressure upon the individual. It does not account for the individual dimension of conscience, which makes it possible for the individual, on occasion, to defy the community, though it does do justice to the social sources of many of our moral judgments. Freud's concept of the super-ego and the cultural super-ego, made necessary by the strictly naturalistic frame of his thought, had the consequence of giving a false account of the increasing tension between the pleasure-seeking id and the demands of an ever more demanding super-ego, as civilization developed. The unnecessary pessimism was fully developed in his *Civilization and Its Discontents* and was expressed in his memorable correspondence with Albert Einstein, in which, incidentally, two creative modern spirits joined issue on the basis of an untenable pessimism and an untenable optimism in regard to human nature. Actually the human self, and not a mythical "id," is creative and destructive on every level of civilization; creative in enlarging the realm of responsibility, destructive in corrupting the realm of values with egoistic taints.

Deficient as the Freudian naturalistic version of the doctrine of "original sin" may be, it has definite advantages over the optimism of the Neo-Freudians who sought to correct his mistakes, chiefly by attributing self-regard to social and historical causes rather than to purely biological ones. The most persuasive of the Neo-Freudians was the late Harry Stack Sullivan ("Interpersonal Psychiatry") who attributed undue self-assertion to lack of security in the self's period of infancy and therefore rightly asserted that the capacity to love was drawn from the security of being loved. But unfortunately this valid scientific analysis of specific forms of undue self-assertion gave rise to rather optimistic efforts to eliminate "self-love" entirely by teaching the "mothering one" to give the infant "uncritical love" (Brock Chisholm). This not only made the poor mothers responsible for all forms of undue self-assertion but persuaded them (if their common sense did not fortunately resist this scientific advice) to spoil the child by indiscriminate and sentimental "love." Karen Horney, one of the most creative of the Neo-Freudians not only derived undue self-assertion from the insecurities of a "capitalistic" culture, but sincerely believed that an adequate psychiatry would eliminate this evil. It is hardly necessary to speak of the even more extravagant optimism of Erich Fromm expressed in *Man for Himself* and developed to the final pitch of absurdity in his *Sane Society*, in which all the rationalistic, optimistic illusions of a Condorcet reappear in psychological garb.

But despite these extravagant forms of pessimism of pure Freudianism and the extravagant optimism of the Neo-Freudians, modern psychiatry has developed a rather more valid account of the relation of self-regarding motives to creative ones, not only than Freudian or Neo-Freudian accounts but than conventional religious or Christian interpretations. It gives a valid account of the endless forms of interpenetration between "ambition" and the sense of responsibility for our neighbors, which must be appropriated if Christian thought is not to fall into either one of the two errors: the liberal Christian error of regarding the love of the neighbor and sacrifice for the neighbor as a simple moral possibility, or the error which infects much orthodox thought, which regards all forms of "self-love" as simply evil. It is, incidentally, not merely polemical distortion which persuades some disciplines of modern culture (economics, for instance) to regard Christian thought as irrelevant because it allegedly thinks it a simple possibility to exchange the "profit motive" for the "service motive." Other disciplines dismiss the Christian interpretation of human nature because they think it implies the doctrine of "total depravity." While this is an error, it is an understandable one.

In short, Christian thought has much to learn from modern psychiatry in assessing the human situation. It must not be deviated from this task by polemical attitudes toward either Freudianism or Neo-Freudianism. We must strive in all humility to enrich the basic insights about human nature, as we have it in Biblical faith, by whatever light may be thrown upon the human situation by any of the disciplines of modern culture. We cannot scorn insights in which truth has been distilled from the half-truths of both Freudianism and Neo-Freudianism, particularly when that truth corrects the half-truths of both Christian pessimism and Christian optimism.

If the psychological disciplines are needed to enrich and correct Christian insights about the relation of love and self-love in the human soul, the disciplines of the social and historical sciences are equally needed if we are to make the love commandment relevant to problems of justice, which have become particularly perplexing in a technical civilization and in a nuclear age. The love commandment is basic both for describing the laws of self-fulfillment of the individual and for describing the ideal harmony of the community. That harmony requires that we do not seek our own but the good of the neighbor. But this ideal harmony can only be an ultimate goal, and cannot be directly relevant to a "sinful" world in which individual and collective self-interests persist in power and where conflicting claims must be arbitrated by some calculus of justice. We need, in other words, a way of making justice the servant and instrument of love, while recognizing that the principles of love are the ultimate norms of human freedom, which cannot be chartered or channeled into any specific law. We need standards of justice not only to arbitrate the conflicting interests of men and nations, but also to define norms for man as creature who is something less than free spirit. He is enmeshed in all the forms of natural life, and these forms and forces, his heterosexuality, for instance, demand moral norms, in which love must be compounded with particular standards, congruent to the mixture of freedom and necessity in human nature. It is, for instance, significant that the norm for the sexual partnership between man and woman should have been spelt out in terms of fidelity to and stability of that partnership. Fidelity is a form of love and the stability of the partnership is meant to do justice both to the intimacy of the partnership, and the interests of the children who are the fruit of the union.

The Christian faith has rigorously held to the standard of monogamous fidelity with very good reason, though it may be questioned whether it is advisable to make the standard of absolute indissolubility so inflexible, when love no longer cements a union which, ideally at least, requires grace rather than duty as its binding force. But a discussion of this detailed problem is premature. We must consider the total problem of proximate moral norms, their sources and their relation to the law of love, if we are to explore the contribution of the disciplines of culture to an adequate Protestant ethic.

Before undertaking this task we must briefly consider the virtues and defects of a Catholic social ethic. Its virtues can be briefly defined as consisting of a sense of the community and of social necessities superior to Protestant individualism; and of an inclination to derive norms of justice from rational calculations or rights, which is superior to either the Biblicism of orthodox Protestantism or the effort to swallow all proximate norms

in the love perfectionism of liberal Protestantism. Its defects are
the too radical separation of the norm of love and the norm of
justice, involving the division of the Christian community into
first class (the ascetics) and second class Christians. The second
defect is that its "natural law" standards of justice are based
upon a classical (Stoic or Aristotelian) ontology. Therefore
they do not provide for the endless, contingent and variable
concretions in history. Catholic natural law is too inflexible to
deal adequately with concrete historical occasions; and this defect is apparent even when modern Catholic theologians make
use of Aristotle's and Thomas Aquinas' suggestion that the application of general rules to particular occasions and contingent
circumstances, must permit a good deal of freedom.

The fact that Catholicism is caught with the absolute standard
of the prohibition of contraception in a neo-Malthusian age,
proves that its natural law is too inflexible for the realities of an
unpredictable history. On another level, the essentially correct
conception of a "just war" evidently contains too precise definitions of the prerequisites of justice. Among these prerequisites
are that the "means of war must be proportioned to the ends in
view." Nothing could be more logical than such a requirement;
but it is rather irrelevant in a day in which we have peace by a
"balance of terror" and cannot afford either to use the dread
instruments or to renounce their prospective use. Significantly
the church does not insist upon this clear requirement of a just
war in our age.

It is not because we are Protestants, rather than Catholics,
that we must dispense with moral norms which rely on deduc-
tions and assume fixed forms and "essences" to guide us in our
responsibilities in the varied configurations of history, but because the circumstances of a technical age shift the essential
conditions of life so rapidly that we must determine the right
action in unprecedented situations by a true analysis of the

factors and interests involved in our choices. In short, we are forced as never before to be thoroughly pragmatic in our proximate norms, holding still to the general standard of the love commandment for our ultimate norm. As religious and moral guides in our harassed and perplexed age, we cannot be wisely pragmatic without availing ourselves of every form of knowledge about the social and economic realities of our national communities and the strategic realities in the international realm. We require not only knowledge of the historic facts but of the standards which have been developed in each form of human togetherness. In the political realm, for instance, the long history of human community reveals that a tolerable justice and harmony can be established only by balancing, deflecting, and harnessing conflicting and competitive interests and, occasionally, by suppressing them in the interests of that total community. We have also learned that politics deals with power, and that power is something more than force. The power of a government is its authority, derived from its prestige, to use force in order to coerce recalcitrant forces and interests. If there is a peril that the political order should encourage cynicism and tempt relativists to make either interest or power ends rather than means, these errors can certainly not by refuted by a sentimental approach to the political realities, which preaches ideals with no relevance to the stuff of history which norms must master. In other words, the moral teacher must know something about the standards which are the stuff of political philosophy.

The problem of economic justice may be even more important in an industrial civilization than those of the political order. They cannot in any case be sharply separated from the latter. Significantly, the course of history in all the healthy democracies has refuted the dogmatism of both the old liberalism and of collectivism. The basic securities of a "welfare state" are the accepted norms of economic life but rigorous "planning" has not proved as effective as a mixed economy. The moral leader must know the reason for this development so that he will not introduce an irrelevant individualism (embodied for instance in the "right to work" laws) or belatedly suggest that it is the function of the Christian faith to substitute the "service motive" for the "profit motive," one of the notes of sentimental moralism in the otherwise creative "social gospel." It is, incidentally, worth recording that the Catholic church, which I have criticized for being informed in its moral judgments by a too inflexible "natural law," has been wiser in guiding the conscience of the faithful about the requirements of social justice in a highly collectivized society, where big government, big business and big labor are necessary evils, than has the Protestant church with its vestigial individualism, inherited from a previous age. The stand of the church on the "right to work" laws, which it rather consistently condemned as incompatible with justice in a mass society, is a case in point.

Next to the issue of economic justice, the issue of racial justice looms as equally important and perhaps more poignant than any issue facing the nation. The primary requisites for facing the issue on the part of the church are loyalty to our basic affirmation of a conception of a common humanity, transcending our ethnic loyalties ("God has made in one blood all the nations of men"); and integrity in standing for the "rights of man" against the pressures of tradition and custom. But it is also necessary to recognize the genuine, rather than purely racist, concerns which inform decent people, who are opposed, for instance, to integrated schools. This requires knowledge about the facts of the basic inherent equality of all races and the historic inequalities, created by the very inequalities of educational opportunities which integration is designed to correct but which cannot be overcome quickly enough to prevent parents from harboring justified fears about the adequacy of the education for their children. On the issue of integrated schools we need empirical knowledge to support and to qualify both the basic universalism of Christian ethics and the religious reservation, succinctly expressed in the words "Judge not that ye be not judged." We must combine ethical rigor with avoidance of the complacent self-righteousness which tainted the anti-slavery cause in the days before the Civil War. The avoidance of self-righteousness is primarily a religious problem and depends upon the religious insight about the involvement of all men in a common guilt. But this religious emphasis becomes formal and empty if it is not implemented by detailed moral and social apprehensions of the complexities of the issues involved.

There remains the final issue, which harasses the conscience of the whole world, for it concerns the ethical and religious dimensions of the cold war and the nuclear dilemma. Any moral guidance on these complex issues of the international situation, must be informed by sufficient historical maturity to avoid at least two dangers. The one danger is to deal with the loyalty of a nation to its own civilization as being ignobly "selfish," and therefore to counsel unilateral disarmament as a "Christian" act of sacrifice in the interest of peace. The other danger is to be heedless of the historical developments on both sides of the Iron Curtain so that we interpret the struggle in purely moral terms as a conflict between democracy and despotism. We ought to have enough knowledge to realize that the Russian system has evolved, not into a democracy, but into an efficient technical civilization of immense attractive power to the agrarian and underdeveloped nations of Asia and Africa. There is furthermore the necessity of understanding both the hazards and the tragic necessity of preserving the "balance of terror" upon which peace is precariously founded. We ought to know enough about the inherent moral ambiguities of the political order to know that this international situation is typical of the

whole political realm and is unique only in the degree of its ambiguity. The nuclear dilemma reminds us in a vivid way that
one of the real tasks of Christian ethics in our day is to accept
the moral ambiguity of the political order, resisting both the
sectarian and the secular perfectionist effort to surmount moral
ambiguity by some simple moralism, but to put this kind of
Christian realism in the service of justice rather than in the service of some *status quo*, as has been the tendency of all Christian
realistic appraisals of politics, whether Catholic, Calvinist, or
Lutheran.

In short, there is no escape from the task of establishing proximate norms of justice to become the instruments of love in the
complex competitions of both the domestic and the international
community. This task can be accomplished in the framework of
Protestant doctrine and the rapidly changing circumstances of
a technical culture, only if theological learning avails itself of all
the disciplines of modern education and culture, particularly the
historical sciences which put us in contact both with the present
facts of modern life and with the perennial and recurring patterns of the political and economic order. If we fail to make use
of these disciplines, our witness to this generation will fall below
that of Catholic Christianity, despite the obvious inadequacies
of its natural law theories.

Pastoral Experience and Theological Training: The Implications of Depth Psychology for Christian Theology

SAMUEL H. MILLER

DEAN SAMUEL MILLER of Harvard Divinity School has come to his present post from a long experience as pastor of the Old Cambridge Church and part-time teacher at Harvard Divinity School and Andover Newton Seminary. He has always been interested in bringing literature and the arts to bear upon the theological understanding of the human personality and its predicament. As an experienced pastor and teacher in the field of Pastoral Theology he has developed a keen interest in, and solid knowledge of, psychodynamics.

INTRODUCTION

WHEN COPERNICUS radically changed man's way of thinking about the universe, transposing the center of things from this little earth to a far-off sun, he unbalanced, in a sense, the structure of space. The psychological reverberations of this event were inestimable. Space had been centered in man and in his particular planet. Now it was dislocated; man himself with his planet was shifted out toward the periphery of things; and with that shift man's sense of his own significance underwent a severe change.

Not only was man let down by the Copernican shift, but there came with it a new conception of space. The universe suddenly opened up with breath-taking vastness. Far beyond anything previously imagined, the interstellar spaces grew to awesome distances. Even a mathematician and a scientist of the magnitude of Pascal could not refrain from expressing his "fright" at this tremendous opening of space.

This historical experience can be described rather simply as the imbalance of outer space. Man was abruptly confronted first with his own demotion from the central point of importance and then immediately shocked by a space of incredible dimensions. Made to feel very little, he was abruptly awed by the endless depths of the universe. The weight of outer space far outweighed his sense of inner value.

This imbalance very quickly became unendurable. The pressure of it forced man to discover resources by which to reassert a balance of power, to adjust inner and outer space, so to speak, in order to approach a comfortable equipoise. The human reaction to the Copernican revolution was that man's inner space was opened up, in order to match the frightening dimensions of outer space. The materials for this operation were at hand in certain tendencies of the Renaissance, in the burgeoning of the modern era, and in the optimism of the Enlightenment and the Romantic movement. All the ancient limits of the human creature so deeply impressed by medieval religion and culture were shattered. Man's mind no longer brooked any limits; his possibilties were conceived to be endless; indeed, it was assumed that perfectibility was well within his reach. The philosopher who had been frightened at such a sudden imbalance of outer space recovered his balance by recourse to man the *thinking* reed.

Probably nowhere is this manoeuvre to redress the balance more clearly described than in the studies by Ernst Cassirer of the Age of the Enlightenment.

> "In estimating the importance of natural science in the genesis and formation of the modern picture of the universe, we must not confine ourselves to a consideration of individual features which science has added to, and by virtue of which it has decisively transformed, the world around us. The extent of these influences seems almost immeasurable and yet it does not fully indicate the formative force which originated in natural science. The real achievement of science lies elsewhere; it is not so much in the new objective content which science has made accessible to the human mind as in the new *function* which it attributes to the mind of man. The knowledge of nature does not simply lead us out into the world of objects; it serves rather as a medium in

which the mind develops its own self-knowledge.
. . . Space and time are extended indefinitely;
. . . *the important aspect of the transformation
does not lie in this boundless expansion, but in the
fact that the mind now becomes aware of a new
force within itself.* [My italics.] All extensive
growth would remain fruitless and could only
lead the mind to a vacuum if it did not acquire
a new intensity and concentration within itself.
And it is this intensity which informs the mind of
its real nature. The highest energy and deepest
truth of the mind do not consist in going out into
the infinite, but *in the mind's maintaining itself
against the infinite and proving in its pure unity
equal to the infinity of being.* [My italics.] Gi-
ordano Bruno, in whom this new climate of opin-
ion first appears, defines the relation between the
ego and the world, between subject and object
in this sense. For him the infinite process of becoming, the great spectacle of the world forever
unrolling before our eyes, is the guaranty of that
deepest meaning which the ego can find only in
itself." [1]

Now the reason I have gone somewhat afield to introduce this
episode of human history is to illustrate what seems to me to
have occurred again in this last century. Freudian research, as
revolutionary as the Copernican discovery, has destroyed the
equilibrium of modern man. Happening in association with
other powerful social and cultural forces, the opening up of vast
psychic spaces deep within man's own center has disturbed his
relationships at every level of his many-faceted life. We have
been brought face to face with imponderable depths in our-

[1] Ernst Cassirer, *The Philosophy of the Enlightenment* (Princeton University Press, 1951), pp. 37-38.

selves, depths of extraordinary potency, capable of the most complicated chicanery, operating at levels far below our conscious control. We now know that we have not been as much in control of ourselves as we thought, and the powers and mechanisms which have determined our character and overt actions were mysteriously beyond our reach for the most part. With something like an X-ray penetration, our most solid convictions and firmest moral ideals were rendered transparent and sight of their inner structure built out of neurotic needs and drives was forced upon us in a series of shaking disillusionments. At the very time when the weight of global contemporaneity accomplished by new facilities in communication and transportation broke upon us in all its confusion, the powerful forces of inner space invaded our conscious minds, our social motives, our cultural propaganda, and our contemporary art, unbalancing once again the equipoise with which men lived in comparative comfort.

To say that such powers have always participated in our many-faceted life of course is true. But never before have they been so generally recognized for what they were. We know now that the conscious life of mankind rests upon a great depth, only partly known, but filled with terrifyingly clever and insidiously deceptive impulses. If the interstellar spaces frightened Pascal by their awesome vacuity, the psychic space of the subconscious is frightening because of its very excess and irresistibly dynamic penetration of the conscious. The weight of this newly opened inner space creates an imbalance of considerable anguish.

Nor is it only that psychodynamics has introduced a new dimension of great power and diversity of structure to the conscious and somewhat overwhelmed mind, but everywhere the conscious now tends to extend its domain, seeping down and coloring the sources of its experience, so that the unconscious isn't quite as unconscious as it was. An area of ambiguity is developing in which the unconscious is being manipulated by the conscious. Turnabout may be fair play or inevitable dialectic, but what consequence it may have in the development of a scientific Machiavellianism or a new and ultra-sophisticated self-knowledge it is hard to say.

In the religious world this imbalance has many profound and radical consequences. A new way to read human nature has been proposed; the center of gravity in man's being has been shifted; the meaning and value of his acts as well as his character are being reconsidered; a more thoroughgoing and sophisticated disillusionment now extends to heights and depths unknown before; explanations of an empirical sort are reformulating the great realities of revelation and grace, reducing them to the frame of contingency. None of the disciplines operating in the articulation of religious reality can evade the thrust of this new factor in man's understanding of himself. Anthropology, Christology, soteriology, the doctrines of the fall, freedom, grace, revelation, and atonement are confronted by a level of man's life rendered transparent for the first time, requiring recognition, evaluation and inclusion in the redemptive process, and therefore in the theological articulation of man's reality.

What this means particularly in Protestant thought can scarcely be overestimated. Since we inherited the powerful iconoclastic forces of the Reformation, and united them with many of the rationalistic tendencies of the Renaissance, we have been almost entirely oriented to the conscious level of man. In doctrinal matters this has led to an almost complete rationalization of dogma, either in liberalism or in various forms of literalistic fundamentalism. Worship has declined, sacrament and symbol have been rendered impotent, while the sermon became the inflated climax of rhetoric and exhortation. In this kind of a situation, the church remains without any tool fashioned to minister to man other than in the region of reason. Yet it is that very region where the severest conflict exists, between the inherited, more or less canonized mythology of the past and the scientific, rationalized mythology of the present.

What inevitably develops is an impossible attempt to solve the conflict on a rational basis. The perennial aggravation and frustration arise because the structures of religious reality transcend the dimension of the discursive reason and thus thwart every effort to resolve the issues on the conscious level. If man is to be saved, his whole being must be involved. Indeed it is in terms of his total self that the religious meanings of symbol and myth become manifest. Not until we understand that the total reality of man extends below and above reason will we find grounds for the rehabilitation of our Christian faith.

But if this is true of the church how much more so is it true of the theological school. There academic discipline is the discipline of analytical and discursive reason. Everything in the Christian faith is reduced to its rationalistic character. Analysis, genetic process, classification, objectivity, descriptiveness—all methods tend to one end, namely, communicable facts to furnish the conscious mind. That this should be so is not strange, but that we should be satisfied that it is so is strange. From time immemorial we have known that one of the inevitable experiences of such a thoroughgoing intellectualization of religion has been the severe crisis of dryness or even of spiritual death, which the theological student endures. One of the great problems we face is how to keep faith viable while increasing its self-consciousness in terms of history or other objective disciplines.

Neither the process of communication in the church nor in the school can be safely reduced to the rational stratum of man. It may be that there are other schools where competence in a chosen profession can be intellectualized, but it is scarcely true of the theological school at its best. Here the communication is not merely a matter of information or of skill, but the development of a religious personality, whose competence will be determined as much by the maturity of his selfhood as by what he knows. This will demand a sharper focus on what a minister is than on what he does; it will raise the old question of his call and fitness for the ministry in new terms; it will reshape the image of the minister to be held by both church and school; and it will require a fresh reckoning with the factors of nonrational conditioning by which a candidate is shaped for spiritual leadership.

Obviously the Protestant school is under a heavy handicap at this point, not merely because of diverse sectarianism, but even more deeply because there is scarcely any tradition of a spiritual discipline in which there are discernible stages toward a Christian norm. Individualism and corrupt forms of freedom run so deeply that resistance immediately is encountered in any attempt to set up a "disciplined community" in which certain sacrifices of personal sovereignty are entailed and a routine of nonrational habit established. Yet to bring into the normal life of the student the resources and possibilities of the subconscious will require something more than lectures and examinations.

PRELIMINARY QUALIFICATIONS

Let us turn now to consider the major implications of this newly opened province for the theological venture in general. Like all young and burgeoning things, it has tended to be a bit brash and impatient. It has sometimes assumed an authority which rashly canceled out nearly all other criteria of truth. Psychodynamics is a new dimension of human reality but it is neither the center of it nor the total measure of it. The afflatus of power and ecstasy of understanding which always come with the opening up of new territory will need to be qualified by a modesty and discipline of its own before it can achieve its appropriate function or contribute its best gifts in the full circle of cooperating arts and skills.

Moreover, if psychodynamics is to take its place in the professional panoply of the minister, a strict assessment of its theoretical character and of its philosophical pretensions must be made. The historic origins out of which it came were so heavily weighted with cultural naturalism that we cannot avoid the drastic examination of its presuppositions and basic philosophy. It is quite evident that recent tendencies make it plain that however restricted to a naturalistic interpretation in the Freudian origins, psychodynamics has found it well-nigh impossible to stay within strict scientific limits.

In the third place, we must consider psychodynamics in the normative mode. From the very beginning depth psychology has developed from a clinical context where neurosis formed the point of illumination. It is not strange that most of the progress in understanding the dynamic structure of the psyche has come from the observation of these critical deviations. Yet this should not blind us to the necessity of forming a sense of the normative, however difficult that may be. We will continue of necessity to attend to the neurotic and its many significant implications for the religious, but even more important in the handling of the complex energies of the religious life will be our vision of the total man in normal operation.

With this in mind, let us consider three general areas where I believe psychodynamics brings a new light and discloses a need for the reorientation of the theological curriculum. Here again I repeat that to a large degree our interests have been monopolized by the negative, the deviants, the neurotic, by which we sought to understand the sick person, or the one in an emotional crisis, or mentally disturbed. This work has its own dramatic urgency and religious significance, and therefore it is not likely to be neglected, and it should not be. But there is a positive and normative realm in which psychodynamics must prove itself or else all religion will seem to be little more than a collective neurosis held precariously in check by a skeptical reason.

The first of these three areas is the new significance of nonverbal communication; the second is the new dimension of the subconscious in all theological construction; and the third is the religious significance of the primary events of life such as birth, death, love, and sin. In these areas both religion and psychodynamics are deeply involved, and their characteristic reflections upon the common situation need to take into account their differing perspectives and values.

THE NEGLECT OF THE NON-VERBAL

Let us lift the first area, which we have called "nonverbal" communication into focus. The most powerful factors in the motivation of human action are not primarily rational or abstract. In one way or another they are concrete, making their appeal as much if not more to the subconscious than to the conscious. The tremendous burgeoning of advertising and commercial art may provoke our ire but it is a monumental witness to the power of nonverbal communication. We may decry the dangers involved in the insinuation of dynamic images, reinforced by repetitious use and associated with slick slogans, but however perverted such a process becomes, it testifies to the potency of subconscious structures far from the rational realm.

If we expect religion to regain its redemptive power, it will need to discover nonverbal means and methods in which the structures of subconscious needs and forces are fused. It is patent that at the present the symbols and rites in which our faith are being expressed in time-honored traditions simply do not communicate, either the revelation of what is divine or the shock of what is basically real. As Martin Buber suggests, there are epochs when the symbols are empty of God's spirit. Or perhaps there are times when man removes himself from the realm where the divine might be encountered.

It is wholly possible that the massive intellectualization of religion in the last three centuries of reason's ascendancy in science, philosophy and education, may have left faith without a witness in the dynamic levels of man's life and being. Like a plant gone to tops, we have no root in the dark depths where sustenance might give us strength to bear fruit. Certainly the growing impotence of sacrament and symbol has been paralleled by the waning of all confidence in analogical pursuit of truth. The rise of scientific objectivity, tentativeness and literal descriptiveness have left all other modes of truth in disdain. It is simply that reality is reduced to sheer factitiousness, susceptible of being apprehended in the net of the conscious mind.

How desperate a schism this may create can be seen in the difficulty of trying to disclose the significance of the cross as the central affirmation of reality to a people thoroughly disabused of all notions of affirmative suffering, or even of discipline, let alone of vicarious atonement. Or again how can the term "redemption" have any meaning in a culture essentially naturalistic, where the solution of all problems is not by the transformation of the human being but by adding conveniences or manipulating technical powers. In so many ways, we may ring the changes on the ancient symbols and rites all we want; there is no answering reverberation in the consciousness of modern man. The radical questions we must ask are whether he is atrophied at this level, or has he outgrown these ancient devices of faith. Merely to increase the intellectual elaboration at the rational level, or the activistic frenzy at the organized level, will do no more than to increase his futility and exhaust his energy. The roots of faith must seek the darker depths of the subconscious. The articulated forms by which he expresses himself must be large enough to hold all the levels of his being in a coherent and meaningful image. It was not Greece who gave us religion. Their contribution was philosophy—the activity of "nous." The Jews were not speculative analysts. They achieved their genius in religion—the wholeness of "sholom."

I do not believe we can exaggerate the fact that we are living at the precise center of Genesis 11—the story of the Tower of Babel. Our world has gone to pieces, precariously held together by the sheer violence of power politics and hostility patterns; its institutions dissimulating a sign of unity by frenzied ubiquitous committees; its symbolic structures in a shambles; the Christian myth which once united it demolished except as a liturgical heirloom. We are no longer born into a world of cultural coherence able to sustain the spirit of man either in community, in faith, or in art. Vladimir Weidle has said that the most significant line of poetry written in our time was penned by Eliot in *The Wasteland*, "I have shored these fragments against my ruins."

And all the while we are laboring in great anguish to construct some kind of unity to pull our world together before it ends in utter chaos and darkness. In such a crisis we are hard at work refining our intellectual machinery, sharpening and elaborating our ideas, increasing in short the very things which cannot by themselves pull the world together. The Greeks were not blind to this dilemma—the Apollonian principle of order did not have the power to produce unity. That was reserved for the Dionysian. The rational is forever increasing the fragmentation of culture; only the symbolic will unite us. By dint of intellectualizing religion, we only increase its divisiveness, until every individual stands alone, finely furnished, it is true, with religious opinions absolutely his own, but quite incapable of achieving any of the integrations necessary for church or community.

Our first necessity then is to reckon with the power and diversity of nonverbal communication. How shall we shock the moribund soul awake? How rehabilitate the limp, strengthless symbols? How shall we train men in the wise use of the concrete reminders of faith? How can the deeper levels of man's being be raised from contempt to participate in the wholeness of faith's action? How can symbolic action and sacramental belief be reinstated in the process of redemption?

The minister in our time has a larger task to perform than merely proclaiming the good news. He must somehow resuscitate the very level of consciousness to which he wishes to speak. He must himself be alive at this level. Truth for him must be indeed incarnate, deep in the flesh. The wholeness of man can alone match the wholeness of saving truth.

And yet it is in this very depth we are strangers. Psychologically we know our way around quite well; religiously we are strangers. We can accept the Oedipus myth and give it viridical relevance, but the Eden myth, or the Isaac myth, or the Christ myth, we find eludes us. For long centuries, and for men wiser than ourselves they opened the gates of reality. Surely we need to find our way again, that the full magnitude of being human may be reflected in the symbols, rites, and myths of faith. Indeed we are not likely to be ourselves, until we understand the greatness of those images which are larger than reason and as timeless as the eternal.

THE NONRATIONAL DEPTHS IN THEOLOGY

The significance of dynamic communication of religious reality carries us directly into the area where theological terms extend far beyond the bounds of strict logic or reason into territory where the light of psychodynamics may throw a helpful illumination.

Take for instance the perennial mystery of the atonement. Worked out in its classical mode, it leaves on all of us an impression of forced logic. Indeed for two thousand years the theories of the atonement have changed from epoch to epoch with a restless and obvious inadequacy. In the realm of the conscious mind there was a great deal unaccounted for, or too much accounted for in juridical terms. I suspect that the reality of the atonement will be disclosed not at the level of the conscious mind, but in the depths of the subconscious where the keys to transference and counter-transference lie, and where the patterns form for new syntheses of psychic energy.

In this same theological area, new work is necessary in the field of anthropology and Christology. The ancient Aristotelian notions of substance eventuating in the Nicean and Chalcedonian creeds with their definitions of the nature of Christ are no longer viable for our time. What we mean by "very God of very God, very man of very man," "The Word made flesh," "God in man," all must be reckoned with now in dynamic terms. The ancient description of "perfection" or "being without sin" must be restated. What is the relation of instinctual drives to that sinlessness? Or of the superego to Messianic hopes? Or of death on the Cross, or compassion to guilt? What problems are indicated by Jesus' anti-familial sayings, or his unmarried state, or his obsession with the Kingdom? What lies behind the miracles or the transfiguration or the resurrection?

Many of these questions obviously are part of the anthropological problem of our time. We do not know what to make of ourselves, precisely because we do not know what to make of Christ. As the "supreme normality" in von Hügel's terms, Christ epitomizes or reveals what man really is. But having lost the relevance of a "substance" metaphysics, we are groping now to reframe the question and seek an answer that will make sense of all the factors which have thronged so tumultously into the making of modern humanity.

Obviously there is no easy answer here. Psychodynamics does

not have the whole answer any more than other segments of man's psyche, but it must be included in the new equation. When E. M. Forster averred in *Howard's End* that modern man was developing in ways which science dare not contemplate and religion would not comprehend, he succinctly pinpointed the problem. The being of man has been extended, ramifying in new directions, opening up vast perspectives and a world environment, and has become extremely powerful, neurotically insecure and anxious, and remarkably sophisticated. Indeed, one of the factors in man's present makeup which works a peculiar difficulty for religion is precisely this very sophistication. Man is capable of existing without many of the illusions which once supported and sustained him. Whether this new adulthood, or as Bonhoeffer called it "Mündigkeit," can be established without canceling out the elemental security of God's love and the promise of an ultimate destiny remains to be seen. Everything now is under the hard glare of the fluorescent light; the shadows are eliminated, the mysteries wiped out.

Man himself of course suffers in this loss of transcendent significance. Confused amid the conflicting testimonies, unable to pull together the hidden drive and the rational ideal, he lurches on trying to make speed or success take the place of significance or integrity. In the realm of religion, he is at once Christian and Freudian, individualist and conformist, naturalist and idealist, materialist and sentimentalist. If he trains for the Christian ministry these strands are seldom discriminatingly identified, but are blessed in a bundle and sanctified in the hope that ultimately God can make something good of all of them, though in most instances the individual is more like the man called Legion than a priest of the all high God.

Our urgency is to identify the total reality of being human. What is the supreme normality, of what does it consist; what are the proper provinces of it, of ego and superego, of reason and faith, of self and community? In a culture like our own, who will label the spurious gospels of our time as poison if the minister has neither the insight nor the courage to do so? We need desperately to know the difference between the Christian faith and the glib heresies which are no more than the sanctified disguises of cultural idolatries.

THE LIFE-GIVING NUMINOUS

If we turn now from the realm of nonverbal communication and the psychodynamic depth of theological constructions, we come to a third area of concern to both religion and psychodynamics. Perhaps I can describe it as the essential health of the soul in maintaining relationship with the numinous. The numinous characterizes those occasions where the power of God is manifested. The avoidance of the numinous, the rising from depth to comfortable superficiality is always at the cost of soul. Religion does not consist in freedom from life. But the subtle task of relating a person to life, especially to those inexhaustible and fructifying levels of life which are characterized by the numinous is indeed difficult.

Fundamentally in psychodynamic terms, a healthy condition of the psyche is maintained by its intimacy with the subconscious. It is this which enriches and reinvigorates the person. In religious terms, the numinous is that area where the divine is felt, where the limits of existence are breached, where love, death, sin, and birth deepen down to mysteries we can only describe as eternal.

Religion has always felt itself responsible for protecting the person from the full traumatic pressure of these events by articulating them in the sacraments. And this it might well do. But there is another responsibility not so generally recognized, of keeping the soul at least close enough to this numinous level so that its resources and dialetic action upon life will not be lost.

How this can be accomplished is far from plain. But it is extremely plain that the culture of our time has almost entirely sealed off these events from our experience. Birth and death are now institutionalized far from affection and sorrow. Love has been biologized, marriage reduced to a convenient legality, and guilt a psychological pathology. Not until we understand how much more important these events are than anything we know about them will we begin to understand that life is itself not a fact, nor a congeries of facts, but something at once more real and more elusive. Nor will we understand that the freer the access of the conscious mind to this rich nuclear liveliness of the numinous the greater the spiritual vigor of a person.

SUMMARY

In the first place, it must be reiterated that psychodynamics needs to be evaluated, theoretically and practically. The tendency to rewrite all religion in analytic terms is fallacious. Psychodynamics is but one aspect of human reality and must learn its place, where it belongs and what it can do. Nothing is more critically needed at the present moment than a definitive study of the relationship of psychodynamic structures to the transcendent realities of theological affirmation.

The recent debate between Buber and Jung indicates the necessity of this basic research. If the subconscious exhausts the meaning of the religious, then the religious in its classical sense has disappeared. If there is still a transcendent reality whence the religious phenomena both conscious and unconscious are born, then religion continues to offer an objective order of reality consonant with tradition. Again we may well discover with such research that any attempt to testify to the reality of the transcendent by recourse to empirical phenomena is balked by the nature of the method. But if this be so, as I suspect it will be, it will only draw the line again between those who want to "condition the unconditioned," to transcend the transcendent, to out-god God and those who confess the tenets of the quiet mind. What would help immeasurably would be a clear discerning study of the distinction between the psychological and the religious.

The second effect on theological training would open all rationalistic disciplines to the questions raised by dynamic psychology. This would mean inevitably some confusion, re-evaluation, and reorientation, but it is inevitable. The patterns of Biblical thought, of church development, of theological dogma, would be illumined by new insight. The structures of worship, of spiritual discipline, of soul care, of conversion, of sacramental and ritualistic belief all would be considered in the light of these new insights.

One of the obvious lacunae in the present communicable knowledge of religion is in the area of phenomenology. Very little has been done since the classic work in comparative religion by Frazer to describe the characteristic structures of the religious life. What Frazer did is not of current usefulness, for our need is not comparative or socio-cultural but phenomenological. What would help us would be a careful and discerning definition of the structures of such fundamental religious experiences as sin, rebirth, forgiveness, repentance, sacrifice. It is significant I believe that the best hope of such clarification seems to be given today by the existentialists. The metaphysic of hope, the exigence of the transcendent, the structures of testimony and witness, and others have already been sketched out provocatively by Marcel.

A word of caution must here be spoken against the temptation of scientific hubris. Over fifty years ago in his Gifford Lectures William James called for a scientific or empirical theology. If these intervening years, with the able but futile attempt of Macintosh of Yale, have taught us anything it is to be skeptical of reducing theology to empirical proportions. Medicine, law, engineering, psychiatry may all be kept within the bounds of limited inquiry and control, but this is impossible in religion. We are dealing primarily with God and His grace, with the transcendent, if you will, the unconditioned, and every pretension of enclosing the equation, or fencing the field of inquiry, rules out the very basic factor that determines its religious character. The more scientific our pretensions the less realistic we become in the religious realm. Religion can never be reduced to clinical conditions, for the simple and profound reason that God is free.

In the second place, we must take account of the general accusation that the theological schools are not preparing men with adequate skills for competent professional practice. Here again we must reckon with an essential difference between professions dealing entirely with empirical phenomena and the ministerial profession which is called to administer the "mysteries" of religion, to affirm the transcendent in the midst of phenomena. We can increase the so-called skills until there is nothing taught but manipulative methods and find ourselves at last with nothing but ecclesiastical mechanics, institutional promoters or moralistic entertainers.

The truth is that the practical skills left to themselves lack a determining principle. They need to be rooted in the historical perspectives of Christian faith. They need to be conscious of the mysteries of the transcendent articulated by theology, both systematic and kerygmatic. They need the criticism involved in the dialectical relationship with contemporary culture. Religious work must always be an uncomfortable struggle between "skill" and the "transcendent mystery of God."

On the other hand, the academic disciplines by which the intelligence is rigorously trained to interpret religious reality in the light of the Biblical origins, historical development and sys-

tematic theology, must maintain a lively, dialetical relationship
with life both in its existential plight and in its contemporary
form.

The traditional disciplines cannot be reduced to pragmatic or
utilitarian considerations. This would betray their essential character and the very contribution they are designed to make as
criteria of the contemporary scene. But if they become totally
enclosed, self-sufficient specializations, then they have betrayed
their usefulness to the minister and to the church, though they
may retain their function in research or in thought. There must
be some way by which the fundamental disciplines of Bible,
history, and theology can be communicated without distortion
to the practicing minister and through him to the needy parishioner. What is dangerously possible if not already in existence is
a Biblical knowledge, a historical sophistication and a theological
elaboration which never gets communicated to the laity in any
shape or form. Indeed these fields of knowledge tend to be mu-
tually unrelated in many theological students. As for a radical
evaluation of the contemporaneous in the light of origins, or
traditions, or an ultimate criterion of truth, this is often ignored.
The problem of the integration of knowledge, of knowledge
with life, and of the student himself is an extremely stubborn
problem. There must be a serious consideration both of the
training program and also of the maturing of the student as a
person. In both instances dynamic criteria and insight may guide
us in bringing a new depth and power back to the educational
program and ultimately to the professional practice of the minister.

The Collaboration of the Pastor

and the Psychiatrist

KENNETH E. APPEL, M.D.

KENNETH APPEL, M.D. is head of the Department of Psychiatry at the University of Pennsylvania and Psychiatrist-in-Chief of the Philadelphia General Hospital. He has given leadership in medical and psychiatric associations and is the past president of the Academy of Religion and Mental Health which he presided over during its formative years. Through his initiative Congress has acted to establish the Joint Commission on Mental Illness and Health, which is currently publishing several monographs, among them one on religion and mental health.

THE SETTING

"Doctor, tell me, is the universe friendly or is it not?" The patient posed this question out of the heart of his fears and phobias. He was community-bound, afraid to travel more than twenty miles from his office and home. There were fears of distance, high places, buildings, elevators, trains, subways and germs. He had frequent nightmares of disaster, threats of death, pursuit by ghosts and demons. Graduated with honors from one of the country's top technical colleges, he was a remarkably successful engineer-industrialist. He had an excellent mind, great ability, and was held in high regard in his city of 100,000. He was on important boards, both business and philanthropic, which molded the life of his community. Brilliant in many ways but suffering from his limiting phobias, his exceptional ability was restricted by his neurosis. His question about the friendliness of the universe was not neurotic; it represented a search for a firmer religious foundation that would reconcile him with life and also, of course, help him to fight his fears. His religious doubts were pretty much existential in origin and nature, his neurosis familially derived. His phobias were unconscious fears of not living up to superlative paternal standards and achievements, and hostility toward a regressive identification with a neurasthenic mother. His doubts about the friendliness of the universe were related to an identification with 18th and 19th century mechanics and science and a dissatisfaction with Calvinistic religious frames of reference.

Psychiatry is the study of emotional and mental disturbances and illness. Religion is one's system of devotions, reverences, allegiances, and practices—whether avowed or implicit, conscious or unconscious. Psychiatry deals with illness—its treatment and prevention. Religion is concerned with the development of the spiritual aspects of personality and the enrichment of personal and social life. Ideally, it should alleviate pain and suffering and help to maintain health. Standards and values, the need to belong, the need for togetherness, the need to feel worthwhile, the desire to be cared for—all of these are important in human life. They are the concerns of psychiatry and are related to religion as well.

Many psychiatrists feel that the fields of psychiatry and religion should be kept separate—that the differences are clearly defined and that mixing them makes for confusion and limits the effectiveness of both. The pastor becomes a poor psychiatrist and the psychiatrist an inadequate religious guide. Some psychiatrists, following Freud and the physics of a previous century, say religion is a delusion consisting of infantile remnants and obsessional defenses. Many clergymen feel that psychiatry is materialistic, identified with an objective science that is not only indifferent but also antagonistic to values. Distrust between these disciplines is therefore frequent. Where such feelings are dominant, the protagonists had better maintain a respectful distance and not spoil the work of each other.

Yet, as we shall note, the area common to the two disciplines is extensive. In one case, a college student, acutely psychotic, was attended by a young psychiatrist who started working on the transference and tried to make the patient express his hostility. The patient became more withdrawn and finally refused to speak. His condition was retrogressing. Raised in a Fundamentalist community, he was suspicious of science, hostile to psychiatry, afraid of the freedom psychiatry would bestow, and fearful that the psychiatrist would try to destroy his religion. The latter was brought up in the school that "takes what comes" rather than systematically exploring, at appropriate times, different facets of the patient's personality. Another psychiatrist then took over who was sympathetic to a religious orientation. Religious understanding represented the first effective step toward recovery and health whereas lack of understanding made the patient worse. By his mishandling of religion the first psychiatrist had wasted three weeks.

It is appropriate that pastor and psychiatrist work together in view of the fact that both are dealing with human behavior and are making efforts to increase human potentialities. Their fields overlap and intertwine—though at times and in some situations it is wise to keep their responsibilities quite separate. It is the purpose of this article to discuss the factors which bear on the possibility of and need for collaboration, and on the knowledge, attitudes and values which underlie such collaboration.

THE SITUATION OF THE CLERGYMAN

Perhaps five per cent of the over 200,000 physicians are psychiatrists. The number of clergy exceeds that of physicians. It would be natural for psychiatrists to expect some help from general practitioners and the clergy. However, it should be understood how unrealistic we are if we expect a great deal of the clergy. Perhaps no profession has so many and such diverse demands made upon it. The minister is expected to be an interesting and inspiring preacher, and to be well informed on theology, literature and world affairs. He should not offend the conservatives in his congregation, and yet he should appear to satisfy the liberals; and he should appeal to the elderly, the middle-aged and the young. He should have enough regard for ritual to please those for whom this is essential and yet he must also appeal to the less formally minded. Some of his parishioners think religion is nothing if not concerned with social work, and so the pastor is called upon to be a social worker. Others feel this secularization diverts religion away from preaching the word of God. The clergyman is required to be not only intellectual but also practical—administrator, organizer, and money raiser. He should be reserved and dignified, as becomes a man of the cloth, yet a good mixer at parties and service clubs. He ought to be a faithful pastoral visitor— to families, hospitals, homes for the aged, orphanages and jails. He must preside at the crucial moments in the life of his community—birth, baptism, confirmation, marriage, community catastrophe, illness, and death. He is expected to act as a marriage counselor and to guide the children of his parish. He may even have psychologists and psychiatrists on his staff and manage a psychiatric clinic! On an inadequate income he and his family often have to make sacrifices in addition to those we have mentioned. His vocation is exhausting physically, mentally and spiritually. He is expected to move with alertness and understanding on different social and cultural levels. Altogether, his task is almost insuperable. It is especially hard for hyperconscientious but inexperienced young clergymen. Some churches and denominations try to solve this problem and help the clergy by having several ministers on the staff of one church, with specialization of function. Others have administrative assistants, social workers, educators and group leaders.

Under those circumstances it is important that psychiatrists are considerate in their demands. However, at times even brief conferences with the pastor can be very helpful to the patient in relieving certain anxieties and giving religious assurance, especially if the pastor is briefed in advance by the psychiatrist.

RELIGIOUS RESOURCES

Readings of a religious nature may be of great therapeutic value. Short daily readings are available that encourage healthy and wholesome meditations. There is a selection of Psalms which has proved especially useful, as have the writings of Joseph Fort Newton on the purpose and practice of religion in daily life. One Christian was helped by Harry Golden's *Only in America* and a Jewess by some brief work of Emmett Fox. A young Protestant mother, on the threshold of psychosis, living promiscuously, deserted by her husband, threatened with the loss of her children and financial support, in despair after three years of intensive psychotherapy and psychoanalysis, was helped by the Roman Catholic *Three Minutes a Day*. This was the only contact she could make beyond the circle of her fears—the touch of another world containing health, hope, forgiveness and spiritual resources, beyond the confines of personal disabilities, suffering, failure and despair. These little readings could be read, underlined, copied, questioned and discussed. It was the beginning of a new line of psychotherapy and help for an almost hopelessly disorganized individual.

There is room and need for collaboration under certain conditions between pastor and psychiatrist. Each has much to learn about the professional needs and expectations of the other. Each must strive to eradicate the indifference or antagonism resulting from his own particular experience and background.

TRAINING THE PASTOR

Extensive studies should not be expected of the pastor. The seminary curriculum would hopefully include courses in the Psychology of Personality and Personality Development, Social Psychology, and the Psychology of Social Relations. Perhaps a course or seminar should be given in the principles of helping others, and specifically counseling and psychotherapy. Practical work in mental hospitals under supervision, with personal conferences and seminars, is perhaps the most concrete way of gaining experience. There are national associations of religion and psychiatry trying to clarify and to some extent fulfill the needs of both professions. The Academy of Religion and Mental Health has prepared a manual with references for study groups. There are many books on the relations between religion and psychiatry and the use of psychology in the work of the church.[1]

ATTRIBUTES DESIRED OF THE PASTOR

The pastor who is of help to the psychiatrist has certain assets. The first of these is his *Person* or *Personality* whose characteristics are warmth, responsiveness, understanding, acceptance, humanity, compassion, benignity, tolerance, forgiveness, love and sacrifice, and the balance that comes with a sense of humor.[2] Next comes *Experience*, by which is meant experience in life, not just in theological schools and mental hospitals. Some people learn from experience what others possess by intuition. *Wisdom* is born of experience. A fourth asset is *Knowledge*—systematic learning and organization of facts and techniques. To knowledge must be added *Skill* and *Courage*. Some of the most knowledgeable young psychiatrists are not by any means the most effective therapeutically. A perspective, a pattern of thinking, a paradigm from which to view people in trouble and try to help them, cannot be definitive,

[1] E. C. Kew and Q.C.J., *You Can Be Healed* (New York, 1954). C. A. Wise, *Pastoral Counseling* (New York, 1951). C. A. Wise, *Psychiatry and the Bible* (New York, 1956). S. Noveck, *Judaism and Psychiatry* (New York, 1956).

[2] J. Gordon, *Your Sense of Humor* (New York, 1950).

only orientative—a springboard for getting into some of the most difficult problems facing society today. *Training* was discussed briefly above.

MENTAL HEALTH

Mental health is the capacity to live reasonably effectively and with considerable satisfaction in the long run. It is a concept made up of many elements such as circumstances, age, opportunities, limitations, and physical health. It is not hard and fast. For example, a person can be in mental health while sometimes being nervous, anxious and in conflict. Even suffering is not precluded. Conversely, pleasure and happiness are not criteria of mental health—that is why the words "satisfaction in the long run" were used, implying something of contentment or serenity even in the midst of suffering, disappointment, failure and frustration. Neither success nor failure necessarily indicates something about a person's mental health. The sound mind in the sound body has been a precept of Western civilization since the time of the Greeks. But the test of a sound mind may be the way it behaves in a sick body. Mental health does not only mean adjustment or adaptation to a society, culture or given situation. It also means trying to change oneself and one's environment. In other words, a person's mental health may be in an unstable equilibrium at different times and under various stresses.

Of the mentally healthy person, however, it may usually be said that in large measure he:

> Has a sense of his own dignity and worth and the dignity and worth of others.
> Is realistic about, but tolerant of, his own limitations and those of others.
> Has the capacity to give and receive love.

> Works with resolution and plays with abandon.
> Has a sense of responsibility towards other peo-
> ple and his community.
> Has a sense of proportion—a sense of humor.
> Acts constructively in the face of trouble,
> without being disabled by excessive emotion or
> panic.
> Has a religious faith, or philosophy, which
> helps him to meet life with zest and to ride out its
> inevitable storms.

It is evident that the characteristics enumerated are more the result of experience and habit than of heredity. They arise from association, identification, imitation and idealism. They are acquired through persons, education, culture and religion. Time is an important element, as is opportunity and fortuity. Example is more important than precept. Unconscious imitation, identification and satisfaction are greater forces than discipline. Rather, discipline itself develops from interpersonal relations, from being involved with people one likes and admires. The endeavors of family life, the school or the athletic field, of the community, church or laboratory, are major sources of mental and community health. Such health involves shared discipline which becomes internalized, in time, as self-discipline. Neither self-discipline, nor the capacity to assume responsibility, nor devotion to others, can come merely from lectures, seminars, books, or stern precepts. As in learning from others, so also in helping others, personal influence is of the highest importance.

ABOUT PERSONALITY THEORY

(1) The *organism* in a state of equilibrium is in a broad sense tensionless, and activity is only metabolic or chemical, and not seen in external muscular movements. This is the antenatal or

intrauterine state, the condition of sleep or anesthesia, of which a great deal is made in some psychoanalytic thinking. It may be considered as a primitive drive expressed in sleep, hypnosis, alcoholic states, trauma, catatonia and stupor, and is thought of in this connection as allied to Nirvana. It is a goal of the psychological process called *regression*. Stimulation excites and disturbs the organism, causing a mobilization of energy which probably, in the earliest phase, represents a primitive fusion of fear—aggression, discomfort—anger. If this stimulation persists, movements result which ultimately, through organized, channeled behavior, develop into the *three types*—toward, against, away from—while the associated feelings and impulses become organized in the great emotions of Love, Hate, and Fear. These are the three elemental feelings and impulses that animals and humans possess in common. Thus, in the case of an excessive, ineffective, dissatisfying or suffering reaction we should ask: Is it primarily Hate or is it Love or Fear that is accentuated—is the impulse Against, Toward, or Away? Many complicated reactions are derived from these three basic impulses in the form of substitutions for them, defenses against them, or attempts at their real or symbolic fulfillment.

(2) The *personality forces* are organized in three chief groups: the emotive and libidinal (Id) as described above; the perceptive, reflective, intellectual (Ego); and the social and moral (Super-Ego). Each of the modern writers on psychodynamics emphasizes especially one set: Adler, the Ego; Jung, the Super-Ego; and Freud, the Id. Heredity is important, as are the anatomical, the physiological and chemical attributes of the individual and the elemental psychological aspects such as sensation, perception, memory and imagination, but experience immediately sets in to produce modifications. Culture, education and religion are important factors in molding the patterns of reaction and expectations. Pavlov emphasized basic physio-

logical conditioning. Freud studied the multifarious conditioning found in the family, then in society, and how the Super-Ego pressures of society and the Id pressures of the emotions are adjusted by the Ego. The Ego is a less powerful instrument of adjustment than we would like to think. There are distinct limitations in the effectiveness of the Ego, both functionally and psychotherapeutically.

(3) The *needs* of people are important in any consideration of the psychology of personality and psychotherapy. They are often not categorized or emphasized in psychiatry, but their fulfillment is crucial for the individual's survival and effective functioning.

Often we expect or demand a certain behavior without having furnished the necessary tools or opportunities. A review of such a scheme of needs is therefore helpful, partly in providing a realistic functional pattern which is often forgotten, partly in offering indications for practical help in therapy. Such help becomes important in view of the great lack of skilled personnel.

There are, first, the primary physical needs for survival such as food, raiment, shelter and everything which contributes to physical health. Second, there are psychological needs:

> Security
> Dependence and independence, in appropriate
>   proportions
> A sense of individuality and self-respect
> Activity, work, achievement
> Creativity, self-expression
> Giving and receiving in relationship with others;
>   social acceptance and contribution
> Change—new experience
> Recreation—play
> Humor
> Devotion—religion

Some, of course, may object to the inclusion of religion under needs, but if we take religion to mean devotion to things, persons, activities and causes beyond ourselves, of a constructive nature for man and society, then their objection may fall away.

Blocking or distortion of needs causes hypertrophied emotions which may appear as disabilities, dysfunctions, illness or disease. If problem solving has been sufficiently developed, skills can often be mobilized to help the person find a way out of his difficulties. But problems that are too severe, too persistent or too numerous can overwhelm the healthiest individual, as combat disabilities have shown.

The importance of child training is, of course, exceedingly evident here. Traditionally, medicine thought of the causes of disease as infection, trauma, toxic factors, deficiencies, tumor formation and deterioration. Psychiatry came along and found many disabilities to be caused by stressful experiences belonging to the past. The chief predisposing causes from infancy and childhood seemed to be overprotection, overdependence, domination, lack of love, exploitation and neglect.

But also the present takes its toll. Loss of loved ones, friends, fortune, financial security, respect, or ability are common sources of emotional illness. Exhaustion—whether in connection with war, or the requirements of vocational and familial duty, or self-driving under the lash of ambition can bring on such illness, as can guilt, domination and loss of identity.

(4) Psychodynamics refers to the psychological, experiential factors influencing human behavior and personality development, as well as to the mental mechanisms or psychological processes themselves, dynamically or motivationally considered. An important concept is that of the *unconscious*.

By the unconscious is meant processes of a psychological nature at work in the person, of which he is unaware and to which he is not paying attention. These processes can be brought out into the open to make understandable what often seems irrational, confusing, contradictory, or foreign in a given personality. The unconscious is a psychological reservior of feelings and attitudes that are relevant to problems and difficulties but disconnected (dissociated) from the main stream of thought. It contains inclinations or aversions that complete the perspective. If an essential part—a significant drive, tendency or attitude—is left out of consideration, the dissatisfaction, suffering, nervousness, or ineffectiveness stands less chance of resolution. For example, the passive, effeminate identification (mother element) may be so strong in a man that he does not have the initiative and aggressiveness to be successful in business. He may consciously attribute his failures to hard luck or unfairness and become discouraged and depressed. He can be helped if his unconscious needs are actively considered, because then he has new stimuli to which he can react in thinking of his problems. But conscious consideration is not the only way this change can come about: also the hurts and setbacks of experience may stimulate him to play a more active role, or he may become fortunately associated with a successful colleague with whom he can identify and thus gradually develop the requisite abilities.

ABOUT PSYCHOTHERAPY

Psychotherapy may be defined as the process of *helping*, or the efforts undertaken *to help, people handle their feelings, motivations and behaviors more effectively*. This concept indicates the broad nature of psychotherapy. It is not limited to words, planned intellectual discussions, reasoning, or argument. In the cure of an alcoholic—with the worst prognosis I had seen, the word alcohol was scarcely mentioned. For a time medication was given for his tremors, pains and insomnia, and vitamins for his nutrition. The focus was on his real interests and goals, looking to their realization, rather than on his failure and frustrations.

People who intuitively spot a person's needs and unobtrusively move into helping, without his being aware of what is going on, have the most success. The association with another stimulates and mobilizes the individual's potentialities so that constructive patterns of activity replace the ineffective and depressing patterns. This happens subtly and unconsciously. The difficulty with so much therapy and counseling is that the helper is tempted to formulate and explain the needs of the sufferer in terms of a system of thought—such as God's will, Freud's libido and other classic interpretations, or the views of Adler, Rank, Jung, Alexander, Horney or Rado. He often meets with resistance. I believe that intellectual formulation and interpretation are less important for the mobilization of resources and certain potentialities than the wisdom and active interest of the helper.

There was a psychotic patient who was desperately ill, lonesome, lost and bitter. She had been deserted by her spouse and children. Sedatives, except in sleep-producing dosages, gave no relief. Despite agitation some communication was possible. She was in a panic. The only recourse was medication for sleep or . . . I went to my office, opened a copy of Thornton Wilder's *The Woman of Andros* and read for one half-hour to her about the heroine Chrysis' reflections on life as she approaches death: "Chrysis raised herself on one elbow and her hands opened and closed upon the cloths that covered her . . . as she said, 'I want to say to someone . . . that I have known the worst that the world can do to me, and that nevertheless I praise the world and all living. All that is, is well. Remember some day, remember me as one who loved all things and accepted from the gods all things, the bright and the dark. And do you likewise. Farewell.' "

In these words were healing. They brought meaning, atonement and forgiveness to my patient. Her healing did not come from understanding the dynamics of her condition but from a shared experience of high aesthetic quality that enabled her to rise above personal sorrow, to accept the pain of universal suffering, assimilate it without bitterness and move on to other areas of normal living and health.

The patient identifies with the psychiatrist's approach to reality, his way of looking at things as revealed through his questions. There are ways of overcoming trouble and tragedy, there are questions that can be answered. The therapist is not perturbed. There are feelings that can be lived through—as in *The Woman of Andros*.

The most miraculous cure of an apparently hopelessly ill psychotic patient of 12 years duration came through the continued daily relationship with another person—not a psychiatrist. The person touched a spark in the patient who was too ill to talk of frustrations, needs, dynamics, and the things usually comprehended under the term insight. But the patient could see and hear things beyond the hallucinations and occasionally would voice some thoughts beyond the delusions. This person's considerate *interest* and continued *presence* ultimately diluted the malignant turgidities of fear and frustration allowing curiosity and friendliness to be expressed. Communication was established, adaptation to simple hospital routines was made and little steps were taken toward collaboration with the social world which had been given up 12 years before. All this gigantic transformation took place before anything like an approach with verbal psychological content could be made! The patient recovered and for years has been a contributing member of society. Non-verbal communication is important with people very sick psychologically. There is a lower, more powerful pre-verbal communication that can often be relied on. The value of silence has been stressed.[3] In human intercourse, what is left unsaid is often more helpful than what is said.

A patient who had been ill with eczema and asthma for twenty-two years had received all the treatment possible both here and abroad. I tried to understand her deeper problems. From infancy she had an asocial, alcoholic and suicidal mother and an alcoholic father. At 22 years of age she had severe attacks of asthma which the allergist thought might cause death. Along with these came the terrific outbreaks of eczema. I said to myself, "What this young woman needs is some sort of security." My chief concern, therefore, was to see her as often as possible and be with her sometimes five minutes a day, sometimes for half an hour or an hour. We talked about everything, about what she had read, what movies she had seen. I tried to build a secure relationship with her. Sometimes she would sit underneath the table like a frightened animal. So I sat down on the carpet beside her and we talked. I thought her essential need was to establish a basic human contact with another individual. Eventually she got well, and I think that without some kind of rational treatment based on an understanding by the therapist of her personality, her experiences and her needs, this might have been impossible. She has been married to an engineer for nine years and they are getting along well. This was social, psychological and emotional therapy. What she had needed most was not physical treatment or drugs but a *secure relationship* with another human being.

Psychotherapy in this instance did not mean explaining to the patient with asthma how she became ill and the physiology of rejection and insecurity, hostility and guilt; it did not mean

[3] D. V. Steere, *On Listening to Another* (New York, 1955).

a discussion of psychosomatic medicine or the influence of the emotions on the body. (Such understanding is far more important for the therapist than for the patient.) It did mean providing a setting for her, an opportunity for growth and the acquisition of security. There was a great release of feeling (abreaction). Much therapy takes place without intellectual formulations and without awareness. Apparently, an unconscious readjustment of the instinctive (Id) and moral (Super-Ego) forces of the individual occurs so that the intellectual or executive (Ego) forces can take over. Psychotherapy is thus a process of conditioning and reconditioning. When the illness is severe, the process takes time and cannot be accomplished by reasoning and brief exhortations.

A process of great importance in psychotherapy is *identification* whereby the patient gradually learns to use the physician's method of tackling difficult problems. In other words, the patient comes to identify with the doctor's scientific, objective approach to situations and conditions which have seemed overwhelming. But the doctor is not overwhelmed. He asks himself, "What are the things to do, what are the possibilities, what has contributed to such identification?" He moves beyond the patient's immediate problems knowing that something can probably be done with this identification. He has a plan of attack which takes the form of asking relevant questions and exhibiting constructive attitudes. The patient finally absorbs this point of view, learning to ask himself the same questions as the doctor and, with repetition and practice, to use the trial and error approach.

In the resolution of conflict between the Super-Ego and the Id we have minimized the power of intellectual functions. These are to a large extent knocked out in the severe neuroses and psychoses and it is therefore futile to hope that they will carry the patient back to health. The sicker the patient and the longer the illness, the less we can rely on the impaired reason and will.[4]

Psychotherapy is not an intellectual exercise; it is an *experience*, and, as such, a process of conditioning and growth. Like growth, much of it goes on unconsciously and automatically. An automatic readjustment of the emotional and social forces (which have been conflicting and in tension) takes place. Psychotherapy is, I repeat, not an intellectual exercise, but a social experience in which the doctor's attitudes toward his patient are the most important levers of therapy.

The doctor should bear in mind the needs of all people: for new experience; for security; for respect and a feeling of individuality; and for responsiveness and understanding from another human being.

Security is given by accepting the patient for treatment, by giving him the support and protection implied in a regular plan of appointments—something to depend on. The physician is not critical and contradictive, or trying to force the patient to change. He shows interest, patience and consideration.

Respect is given by affording the patient a feeling of individuality and worth. The doctor accepts the patient for what he is, with all his annoyances and immaturities. He allows freedom of expression without condemnation or criticism. He is tolerant and permissive. He recognizes areas of responsibility and irresponsibility (due to chance, training, past experience) as part of the patient's condition.

The physician shows responsiveness by making efforts to

[4] At times, with even rather intense disturbances, it is possible to comfort a patient with definiteness, "Now this is the situation. These are the things to do." Then give the person concrete suggestions, direction, and probably also medicines. Yet, complete directions will not solve the majority of problems. Patients have had plenty of advice from their family doctor and relatives, and they have tried to reason for themselves. What they need is the oblique approach of the kind discussed.

understand what forces are at work in his patient. These efforts are often more important therapeutically than actual
understanding. General practitioners, therefore, can do good
psychotherapy without a profound knowledge of psychopa-
thology.

Experience has unconsciously produced blocks and distortions in the majority of cases. New experience, therefore, is
required to restore the emotional homeostasis. Planned new
experience—which may be called psychotherapy—consists in
setting the stage for reducing fear and anger to constructive
and realistic proportions.

Psychotherapy appears to me as a creative social experience
allied to aesthetic experience, in which opportunities are af-
forded for: (1) releasing the latent life and growth impulses
(eros, libido, elan) of the individual; (2) lessening the destructive forces of excessive fear and hate, thus (3) allowing the
creative forces to express themselves again through intellectual,
realistic, and social channels.

This process of reorganization, then, is largely unconscious,
at least in its earliest and critical stages. In the most severe
disturbances, whether neurotic or psychotic, the malignant
emotional intensities and defenses prevent rational communication between physician and patient, and yet improvement is
possible. By infinitesimal growth in an appropriate environment, constructive impulses rise to the surface. The therapist
attempts to repeat the conditions of the child's normal wholesome development.

The patient thus becomes a partner in therapy, a collabora-
tor with the therapist in the search for health, prospecting
the areas of phantasy, imagination, impulse, feeling, emotion,
and the physiological, visceral and skeletal responses and
activities. The primitive personal drives may have carried the
patient far into the infernal regions, and all the therapist can

do is report and share this experience. His presence, interest, kindly questions, and his obvious identification with all the suffering, enable the patient to carry on. It is this *unflagging effort* that brings healing.[5]

Insight on the part of the patient is sometimes valuable. However, in some psychotic, prepsychotic, or severe neurotic conditions, it may be tragically destructive. In general, the therapist feels that if there is insight there is less likelihood of recurrence. However, many patients have insight but no cure. The greater number, I believe, have cure without insight. There are instances of spontaneous cures. The paucity of insight in many patients who have been improved or cured has impressed me. Insight, it seems, is more often an *indication* of improvement than a tool of therapy.

The aesthetic experience in art, in literature, in life, in psychotherapy, has validity, as does the intellectual. The therapeutic experience has much in common with the aesthetic. A therapeutic hour gives the patient and the therapist a creative experience, not unlike that of Lili in the movie, who was not saved by reasoning, but by constructive human contacts. On the ladder of self-destruction she responded to the puppets' interest, to their wanting her to participate in activities, to their insistence on going along with her when she tried to leave. Interest, participation and creative contact saved two lives. It was not reasoning and intellectual understanding that accomplished the healing.[6]

A brief working knowledge of psychiatry is indispensable to the clergyman. He will understand more adequately the many

[5] In his essay on Faust, Santayana gives a description not only of Faust but also of the experience that every psychiatrist has with desperately ill patients.

[6] K. E. Appel, "The Present Challenge of Psychiatry," presidential address, *American Journal of Psychiatry*, Vol. III, No. 1, July, 1954.

motivating forces of human behavior, the factors responsible for social ineffectiveness, delinquency, neurosis and psychosis. He will understand the guidance needed in the relief of suffering, and in the correction of deviations and ineffectiveness. He will broaden his view of man and human relationships, and deepen his well-spring of compassion, benevolence and wisdom. He will become a better family counselor and, in this way, share in the preventive work of community education on mental health and illness. He should in certain instances be able to help the psychiatrist in his work with the most neglected people in our society, the mentally ill. He, in turn, could hope to get more help from the psychiatrist in community activity, group work, community education, and social psychiatry, and persuade him to be less preoccupied with the individual patient. He could stimulate the psychiatrist's concern for mental health (rather than morbidity), for the cultivation of creativity and the principles of leadership. Together they could then look toward the building of sound communities. Collaboration would increase the effectiveness of each in his chosen profession, without the one usurping the function of the other or displacing him.

Pastoral Counseling and the Ministry

SEWARD HILTNER

SEWARD HILTNER is Professor of Pastoral Counseling at the Federated Theological Faculty of the University of Chicago. Three volumes on pastoral theology and pastoral counseling bear witness to his attempt to enrich pastoral counseling with the insights of Carl Rogers' psychology and implement traditional forms of theological education with adequate instruction and training of future ministers in the area of pastoral psychology and pastoral counseling.

PASTORAL COUNSELING is that aspect of the minister's direct help to individual parishioners and families that includes the following conditions. First, the parishioner recognizes a need and is prepared, although not necessarily in clear-cut fashion, to acknowledge it. Second, he recognizes that at least some of the need lies within him, however much that part may be complicated by external circumstances. Third, he assumes some kind of initiative in seeking help from a pastor, although this may mean his responsiveness when a pastoral call is made upon him and not necessarily his making a trek to the pastor's study. Fourth, he is prepared to accept the role of the pastor, at least in some measure, as helping him to help himself, rather than serving as a *deus ex machina* that will solve his problem for him. When these conditions are present, although not necessarily without ambiguity, then what follows is pastoral counseling.

Our definition of pastoral counseling, it may be noted, is purely functional and operational in nature. It says nothing about whether the counseling is good or bad, based on solid theological premises or none at all, psychologically informed or ignorant. That seems proper for a functional definition.

We may call attention also to the fact that all four of the conditions stated as necessary for pastoral counseling are about the parishioner. When he has a need for counseling, acknowledges that need, is receptive to a pastor's help, and accepts a conception of that help that retains his own responsibility in the process—then pastoral counseling takes place. In putting the matter in this way, we are of course assuming that the attitude, knowledge, and skill needed in the pastor are already present, awaiting only the necessary conditions in the parishioner. To put it in another way, pastoral counseling is practiced when a parishioner needs and wants it, not when the pastor decides he wants to perform some counseling.

Since we are eager to have a general definition of pastoral counseling that is purely functional in nature, we note again that the counseling that follows the presence of the four conditions may be good, bad, or indifferent. Even if the pastor simply gives the parishioner the "brush-off," that is an instance of pastoral counseling provided the four conditions were present in the parishioner. To be sure, such an instance would be very bad counseling indeed. But it is necessary to put the matter in this way in order to prevent any pastor from saying that he does no pastoral counseling. The pastor does not, except in an indirect way, control the emergence of the conditions that lead to counseling. What he does control is whether he does the counseling well or badly. But by our definition there can be no non-counseling pastors.

From this definition it follows also that not all the pastor's personal contacts with a parishioner—not even all those in which helping is the central aim—may be viewed as counseling. On the one hand, there are such contacts in which the dominant functional aim is something other than helping or, to use the ancient metaphor, "shepherding." Communicating the gospel or fostering understanding of Christian truth, and organizing and "cohering" persons within the fellowship—these are thoroughly legitimate dominant aims at the proper occasions, not contrary to the aim of helping but different from it.

On the other hand, not even all shepherding is pastoral counseling. The parishioner may be unable to acknowledge his need. Or even if he admits a need, he may not recognize that part of it involves his own person. Or if he realizes that fact, he may not regard a pastor, or this pastor, as a trustworthy helper. And even if all three of the above conditions are present, it will not be counseling if the parishioner refuses any element of initiative or responsibility in relation to the helping process.

From the point of view of pastoral counseling, the pastor's attempts to mediate help to people when some of the counseling conditions are absent may be viewed as "pre-counseling pastoral work." What the pastor does at various stages prior to counseling may have much to do with whether counseling, as needed, is eventually begun. In this indirect sense the pastor does bear some responsibility for the eventual emergence of the conditions in the parishioner that are necessary for counseling. But he can only help to develop the soil; he cannot create the plant.

An accurate model of the relationship between pastoral counseling and the various forms of pre-counseling pastoral work must be drawn in the form of a continuum, not as a collection of compartments. In such a model we may place pastoral counseling at one end of the continuum line. When all four conditions are present in clear-cut fashion, then the process that follows is pastoral counseling. When the conditions are present but in more ambiguous fashion, we still have pastoral counseling but not so close to the end of the continuum.

At the other end of the continuum we would have the complete absence of all four of the stated conditions despite the existence of a need for help. In between the two extremes we should find the overwhelming majority of the situations in which a pastor tries to mediate help.

If the continuum model is accepted as an accurate representation of the relationship between pastoral counseling and pre-counseling pastoral work, then one more conclusion follows which is important for our further study. If there is, as the continuum implies, a connection between one point and another on the continuum, then anything we learn by studying a situation at one point can also shed some light on another point —provided we have located the two points. The study of clear-cut instances of pastoral counseling is, therefore, not the sole way in which light may be shed on pastoral counseling. We may study attempts to mediate pastoral help at any point on the continuum, and draw legitimate conclusions about both pre-counseling pastoral work and pastoral counseling itself.

In moving toward our larger subject, the place of pastoral counseling in the ministry, we shall begin with an actual instance of a pastor's attempt to help a parishioner. Using our continuum model, this situation does not rest at the counseling end of the line but is perhaps two-thirds of the way in that direction.

CONCRETE PRACTICE

A man of early middle years, whom we shall call J. L. Lathrop, is a member of the church of which the Reverend Robert Mennen has been a pastor for a few months. Young Mr. Mennen is continuing his formal graduate education on a part-time basis even though he has been graduated from a theological seminary and is ordained. Before the contact with Mr. Lathrop that will be reproduced here, Mr. Mennen had known him only "casually," as he described it. He knew that Mr. Lathrop was active in one or two church groups, and that his occupation was salesman. He had felt Mr. Lathrop had a "friendly kind of way" about him. But there had been no previous personal conversation.

One evening, after both Mr. Lathrop and Pastor Mennen had attended a meeting at the church, Mr. Lathrop approached the pastor in the corridor and asked if he might drive him home. Since the pastor had relinquished his own car to his wife for the evening, he was pleased to accept this free taxicab service. As soon as they got into Mr. Lathrop's car, the conversation then took place that is given below. It was set down by Pastor Mennen upon his return home. It is probable that the actual conversation was three or four times as long as this reproduction. But since the pastor had had previous experience in recalling verbatim conversations, it is likely that his account is accurate to the main points although compressed.

MR. LATHROP: The main reason I offered you this ride was
1   to get a chance to talk over with you a problem that has arisen in our family.

PASTOR MENNEN: If I can help you to see this problem more
1   clearly, I'll be more than glad to listen.

MR. LATHROP: (*With an air of plunging in*) Our daughter,
2   Sue, became engaged to a young man this spring, with our permission, but with the understanding that the marriage was not to take place immediately. Now they want to be married next month.

PASTOR MENNEN: I see.
2

MR. LATHROP: I've no objection to the boy at all. He seems
3   to be a fine lad, and I've known him for years. But I've asked them to wait until this Korean war situation has cleared somewhat. He's just 21, and although he has seen some military service already, that's no guarantee that he won't be called back in.

PASTOR MENNEN: Your feeling is that you accept the boy, but
3   that the war situation is reason to go slowly regarding the actual marriage?

MR. LATHROP: That's it exactly. And yet there are a couple
4   of things more that make me urge them
to wait. This boy, George, comes from a
broken home, and he has never really known
a decent home life. So the kind of life that
Sue has in our home is undoubtedly attractive to him. Then this summer Sue came
home one night, and I could tell from her
manner that there had been some kind of
difficulty. She admitted that they had had a
fight and that she had given the ring back
to him. But he had thrown the ring away
angrily and had driven away. Later he got
back into her good graces and admitted that
he hadn't really thrown the ring away but
merely pretended to. This seems pretty childish behavior to me; so I'm not sure that these
kids are ready for the responsibilities of marriage.

PASTOR MENNEN: This indication of immaturity, plus the war
4   situation, combine to make you urge them
to wait?

MR. LATHROP: Yes, that's it. (*Silence for a moment*) But
5   that's not the whole story. (*Rather tempes-
tuously*) This problem is actually splitting up
our home. Josephine, my wife, came from
a German family where her father's word
was law; and consequently she wants to see
to it that Sue isn't so tied down as she was.
So Sue and her mother are on one side
against me, and George just says enough to
keep the feelings high on both sides. I've

tried to point out to them that I have no objections to the marriage, but that I just want them to wait until things have settled down a bit. But they seem to have no respect for the judgment of their elders.

PASTOR MENNEN: I see. You not only are concerned with the
5 possible effect of the war situation on the marriage, but also with the preservation of a happy home life of your own?

MR. LATHROP: That's it. Of course I could give in to them.
6 (*Then thoughtfully*) But I'm not sure that I'd feel right with myself about it if I did. If I could only convince them that by waiting a few months they could ensure their own happiness, and that of my wife and me besides. It looks as if that is what I should concentrate on doing.

PASTOR MENNEN: It looks to you, then, as if the real nub of
6 your problem is to maintain a peaceful home of your own, and that in order to do so this problem of the marriage of Sue and George must be faced satisfactorily?

MR. LATHROP: I think so. Well, thanks for your time. I
7 know I've made you late at home; so blame it on me if your wife bawls you out.

PASTOR MENNEN: Not at all. I hope that the problem is clearer for you. Many thanks for the lift. Good night.

What really took place in this pastor-parishioner contact? To what extent was needed help mediated? What can our analytic reflection upon the contact suggest about pastoral counseling? About pre-counseling pastoral work?

We may begin by examining Mr. Lathrop in the situation. And the first thing that strikes us is the delicate balance between wanting and not wanting help, which he exhibits straight off. If he were ready for help in an unambiguous fashion, he would have called for an appointment with Pastor Mennen, or have come round to his office. Instead, his approach was indirect. He came to the pastor after an evening meeting at the church, and offered to drive him home. In the automobile situation the two would not sit facing each other; and besides, as driver Mr. Lathrop would have something for his hands and feet to do while he talked. He wanted some help; but these things suggest to us that some indirection was necessary in his asking for it.

When Mr. Lathrop gets in the car, however, he says forthrightly that he wants to discuss a family problem. He does not talk for twenty minutes about the weather or driving conditions or other impersonal matters, but sets himself to talk about his problem. There has been an indirect approach previously; but once he and the pastor are together, Mr. Lathrop makes a direct attack on his problem. We do well to see some ambiguity here about securing assistance, but with the balance thrown on the positive side at the crucial point. By the time this point in the contact is reached, it is clear that Mr. Lathrop recognizes he has a problem and wants the pastor's help on it. It is uncertain how much, if any, of the problem he feels lies within him. And precisely how he conceives the pastor's function of helping is still also unsure. Noting these remaining ambiguities, any pastor dealing with Mr. Lathrop would be wise to avoid pushing or anything else that would make Mr. Lathrop feel guilty because his desire for help is still clouded and mixed.

In Mr. Lathrop 2 the first clue is given as to the content of the problem. His daughter wishes to advance her wedding date. From the fact that there is a problem to be discussed, and that Mr. Lathrop says it relates to his daughter's marriage, we might justifiably infer that he is opposed to the advance in the date of the wedding. But he does not say so. That is, the first statement about the content of the problem is made neutrally, which is not the same as if Mr. Lathrop had said, "I'm opposed to a change in the plans we agreed to." That is, Mr. Lathrop's ambiguity continues. He is going to discuss the problem, but will reveal his own feelings about it only slowly and under certain conditions.

Mr. Lathrop gives the first statement of feeling, in an indirect fashion and accompanied by a "reason." Indirectly, Mr. Lathrop says for the first time that he does not want the wedding date to be advanced at least to the extent the young people desire. And as reason for this desire on his part he presents the war situation. The young man might be called again into active military service. The feeling or conviction is presented concomitantly with a reason or justification. This reason is one that would receive a high degree of social acceptance. If Mr. Lathrop stopped various people on the street and explained that he wanted his daughter to delay her marriage a bit because her fiancé might be called at any moment into active military service, the great majority would believe his reasoning made sense. Mr. Lathrop has not thought out consciously that he will present first the reason with the largest probable degree of social acceptability, but that is what happens—as, indeed, it does with us all.

At this point in the contact a very striking thing happens. In reply to Pastor Mennen 3, Mr. Lathrop says, "That's it exactly," which means he believes the pastor has understood what he has been saying. But he adds, ". . . and yet . . ." Mr.

Lathrop then gives two more reasons for delaying the marriage. The nature of the first is not altogether clear but is partially so. George came from a broken home; and because of that he may be all the more interested in a stable home like Sue's than would otherwise be the case. The implication in Mr. Lathrop 4 is: is George interested in a stable home, or in my daughter as a person? Clarified, the majority of people would probably agree that Mr. Lathrop had a point. But some would say, "What's wrong with wanting a stable home life?" The probable social acceptability of this reason is high, but not so high as the military service.

The next reason is quite clear in content: the young couple has demonstrated some childish characteristics. Clear though it may be, this reason actually has less probable social acceptability than either of the others. Many would say, "Spats by young lovers are routine; forget them." Or, "Be glad George didn't really throw away the ring."

Mr. Lathrop is peeling the onion. He is taking off one layer of "reasons" after another, in decreasing order of their probable social acceptability. And this process becomes even clearer in Mr. Lathrop 5. The first three reasons involved only the welfare of the young couple for their own sake. Now emerges reason number 4, which is of a different order. Mr. Lathrop's wife is aligning herself with the young couple and against him. We may note that this is set forth ambiguously, that the admission of a vested interest of his own is made only indirectly, and that he concludes ". . . they seem to have no respect for the judgment of their elders." Mr. Lathrop does indirectly admit the taint of ego-involvement. He may indeed want very much the happiness of his daughter. But his own interest is also involved in the marriage timing decision. But this reason is far less likely to prove socially acceptable than any of the three previously presented. So, naturally enough, it comes last. The onion has been peeled far enough to reveal self-interest, but that interest is immediately clothed lest its nudity result in rejection.

At this point we may return to ask what the pastor has done in this conversation. It is our conviction that, through Mennen 5, this pastor, in spite of some technical errors and some stiltedness, did actually convey to Mr. Lathrop at each point his understanding of what Mr. Lathrop had been trying to communicate to him. Those unfamiliar with this process and reading the dialogue hastily might wrongly conclude that the pastor merely parroted what Mr. Lathrop had said. In the first five responses, what the pastor actually did, in effect, was to imply on each occasion, "Now, let me see if I get what you've been trying to convey to me. The best way for me to do this is to give you my version and let you correct me if I'm wrong. As I got it, what you meant now was so and so. Did I understand you correctly?"

Those who want to know whether it is ever in place to do something more than convey understanding may, after a fashion, be reassured. Once a counseling relationship is firmly established, it may make much less difference who says what because, if the wrong thing is said, it may be rejected without rejecting the one who says it. But especially in the early stages there is absolutely no substitute for doing one's utmost to try to understand what the other is conveying, that is, to get as far inside his frame of reference as he is willing to permit. At a glance this may appear somewhat passive. But look what it produced in the present conversation.

Mr. Lathrop began ambiguously. He said he wanted to discuss a family problem (Mr. Lathrop 1), but his first statement about its content was neutral in regard to his feelings on it (Mr. Lathrop 2). He gave a clue to his view indirectly, but attached to this a reason that few would refuse (Mr. Lathrop

3). As Pastor Mennen continued, in his responses 4 and 5, to try to understand and accept what Mr. Lathrop meant, the latter found it possible to unpeel additional layers of his onion. This unpeeling was not an automatic or inevitable process. It could have been arrested at any point.

Suppose Pastor Mennen 3 had been like this, "But if he's been in the service already, he isn't very likely to be called back, is he?" Even if the pastor's inference is far more objectively correct than Mr. Lathrop's, much would be lost by such a comment. If even a socially acceptable reason is met by argument, Mr. Lathrop would be most unlikely to go on to the other orders of justification that are less probably acceptable. Or again he might have said at Pastor Mennen 4, "Now wait a minute. Surely you can't hold it against the boy himself that he comes from a broken home, especially when this experience has made him value a stable home life. And as to these lovers' quarrels, tut, tut, I've had them myself." We can be sure that the unpeeling of the onion would have stopped after any such response. We conclude, then, that whatever might be appropriate in later stages of pastoral counseling relationships, at this time and this stage anything except the genuine expression of understanding would have impeded the process.

There is an interesting confirmation of this in what takes place between Mr. Lathrop 6 and Mr. Lathrop 7. At 6, Mr. Lathrop is consolidating and clarifying what has been brought out previously. The course he is going to follow has no guarantee of success, but he is now clearer than before that he should make the attempt, not feel guilty about making it, and not make his effort dependent upon an advance assurance of success. Then in Pastor Mennen 6 the pastor pushes Mr. Lathrop. It was not so much that he failed to understand what Mr. Lathrop had been communicating. That would have caused no harm if he had checked up on himself. The error was in shifting his gears entirely, doing something quite different from what he had done at any previous point—and being unaware of the difference. The result was that Mr. Lathrop took the immediate occasion to close the discussion. And perhaps even his word about the pastor's wife issuing a reprimand is not without significance.

In summary, then, we see a parishioner who, despite his mixed feelings about beginning at all, does get up his courage and plunge into his problem, but who starts with those things about which rejection is least likely. So long as the pastor proves ready to understand and to try to grasp how he sees the situation, Mr. Lathrop unpeels several successive layers of his feeling about the problem, each less flattering than the last. But the minute the pastor moves beyond what Mr. Lathrop has been trying to convey, the latter retreats. Up to this point, we believe real help was given; and that help was not negated by the bad mistake. But without the mistake, or if the mistake had been recognized and acknowledged, it is probable that the discussion could have achieved further clarification for Mr. Lathrop.

PSYCHOLOGY AND THEOLOGY IN
PASTORAL COUNSELING

Even though our analysis has been brief, it has already suggested in principle the place of psychological understanding in pastoral counseling. We saw Mr. Lathrop's initial dividedness about getting help, and his caution as he proceeded about how much he would reveal. We saw that the pastor's understanding acceptance of him at each point of the revelation enabled him to proceed to a deeper layer of his problem, potentially more capable of self-critical evaluation. In accepting the expressed feelings and convictions, the pastor did not find it necessary to agree with them. But they were not causes for critical rejection from the outside, i.e. from the pastor. The exception came, we noted, near the close of the contact.

As the study of what is going on within a person, or between persons, psychology is an immensely valuable aid in pastoral counseling. It enabled Pastor Mennen to recognize that something of a very constructive nature was going on within Mr. Lathrop despite the negative feelings he was expressing. It has helped us to grasp the successive lowering of the layers of ego defense (peeling the onion), to see the ambiguous forays and retreats in which Mr. Lathrop engages, and finally to see that the active participation of Pastor Mennen was vital in the emergence of Mr. Lathrop's new perspective upon his problem.

Let us be certain that we understand the absolute necessity of psychological understanding in pastoral counseling. Nothing could have taken the place of a grasp of how the ego defenses work, relaxing slowly when not attacked, freezing when they are. A pastor who thought he did not use psychology in this sense would simply be using bad psychology. For good or for ill, some psychology is involved. Our plain task is to see that it is more adequate.

What of theological understanding in the contact with Mr. Lathrop? Unlike much pastoral counseling, there was nothing explicit in the content of the Lathrop interview that drew upon explicitly religious or theological matters. But theology is there and in two senses; first in understanding the meaning of the contact in a deeper way; and second in giving clues about further practical helpfulness. Whether any of this was clear to Pastor Mennen is uncertain. We speak now of our own reflective analysis.

Why are we concerned in principle to respect the serious communications of another person, as the young pastor however imperfectly attempted to do in this case? To be sure, like Mr. Lathrop we may have layers of reasons. The top level may be pragmatic, simply because it works better. A second level may be projective prudence. We recognize empathically that if we were revealing ourselves to another we should want him first to see what we meant rather than go riding off in all directions. At a third level we encounter the idea of otherness, of Thouness, respected for its own sake and not because it is a prudential safeguard of our own complexities. But finally, Christian thought alleges that we respect our neighbor because he is a creature of God who, despite his sinfulness like our own, has nevertheless been made in the very image of God. Not to respect is to degrade; to degrade is to blacken the very image of God.

There is a good deal more that theology can do to help us grasp the underlying nature of the Lathrop-Mennen situation. Mr. Lathrop is a good typical sinner. The closer he comes to a recognition of his own ego-involvement or perverse self-centeredness, the more skittish he becomes about going on. He never quite acknowledges the extent of this interest. But to the extent that he does, to that very extent is he released—not from the general fact of self-interest but from a preoccupation that makes the selfishness of an interest unexaminable and hence in no respect correctable. And yet we note that sharp words about self-interest would have had only negative results. Instead, acceptance and understanding preceded truer critical self-judgment.

Religion and theology, and their implications for all dimensions of human life and thought, come often into the explicit content of pastoral counseling. But even when, as in the Lathrop interview, they do not, there is much that can be understood on a deeper level only as a theological perspective is brought to the examination of the encounter. Although we have hardly exhausted the subject, we have briefly illustrated it. For the Christian pastor engaged inevitably in counseling, it is essential that both a psychological and a theological perspective be brought to bear upon the situation and his participation in it. Neither can take the place of the other nor replace the other. In our view, they are not two realms but two perspectives and two contexts.

OLD AND NEW IN PASTORAL COUNSELING

It is our contention that some of the necessities of pastoral counseling are deeply imbedded in the tradition, that others were understood inadequately or not at all by the tradition, and that it is our task to separate one from the other. This process is not aided either by those who believe there should be nothing new in Christian practice or by those who believe the less said about our predecessors the better. We shall attempt a summary statement of some of the principal contributions old and new.

The first of the traditional insights is about the importance of concern, respect, or Christian love in relation to the person we try to help. No technique or method can ever take the place of such a positive inclination, ultimately based on the person's being a child of God and our brother but proximately resting also upon consideration of his individuality. Modern study confirms and reinforces this traditional wisdom.

Second, the tradition rightly teaches that the most we can ever do in helping another human being is to mediate rather than to give something. The deeper the help, the clearer it is that we did not create the help nor the means to it but only contributed to their discovery.

Third, the ability to respect the otherness of another, to love his Thouness in the Christian sense, is finally a gift even though that gift, once recognized as such, may also be cultivated. We may love because we have first been loved. We can accept and understand otherness because our own otherness has been accepted and understood.

Fourth, our helpfulness is intimately related to our availability. No matter what kind of help we are equipped to give, we fail if we are not alert to need when it exists, according to the principle of the Good Samaritan or the shepherd seeking the lost sheep.

Fifth, the pragmatic success of our help can never be ultimately divorced from our understanding of the context in which help is a possibility. Whether we talk about God may in this situation or that be of lesser importance. Whether we are aware of God's presence is always of first importance.

When we turn from the old to the new insights, it is tempting to suggest that the latter deal with method while the former are about aim and motive. There is real truth in this, but the statement may nevertheless be misleading. For the kind of method discovered by the new is not mere technical apparatus; it involves something very close to the roots of one's attitudes and motives.

The most striking new insight is about dealing with negative and ambiguous feelings. These are to be accepted and understood, not overtly and verbally resisted, precisely because it is acceptance and understanding that may make them release their demonic power. We should have known this. The Psalmist and Job and Jeremiah were familiar with it. It is a logical implication of the traditional principles, once we see its significance. Nevertheless, its full significance is a new discovery.

Second, we have new insights on how to respect the otherness of another. If we have the patience, and some skill, he will reveal this to us. If we assume that our common creaturehood enables us to read ourselves into him, being either blind to or judgmental against what is unlike ourselves, then our profession of respect for otherness is swallowed up by our distortion in practice.

Third, if we are mediators and midwives rather than creators and contrivers, the modern insight helps us keep this primal fact steadily before us and thus improves our therapeutic effectiveness. The basic insight revolves around the ways of self-examination by the pastor of himself in professional relationships. Self-examination is not new, but the ways of doing it through reflection on counseling relationships are new, and most helpful.

The fourth new insight is about the layers of ego-defense in the human person, with all the implications they have for counseling. We saw a series of such layers begin to be unpeeled by Mr. Lathrop. In all illness or misbehavior we now see two kinds of factors: some sort of positive intention trying to protect something worth protecting, and a negative result because the means used bring additional problems. But if even the worst illness contains some positive intention, the negative result cannot be entirely foreign to therapeutic efforts. There is no minimizing of the difficulty and even, on occasion, of the practical irreversibility of the problem. But the belief in a positive intention is a powerful tool of actual help.

The fifth new insight is that some people can give better help to some people on some kinds of personal problems than pastors can. As mediators of help on personal problems, it is only in the present century that psychiatrists, pediatricians, clinical psychologists, social workers, educational counselors, and others have been present to perform functions which previously were either performed by the clergyman or were not performed at all. We are now very far from a day in which it was assumed that the pastor was the one person who could help about anything you couldn't put your finger on. This is a very good thing in two ways: first because more help is being mediated to more people who need it; and second be-

cause it is compelling pastors to define their own function
more precisely.

There are some aspects of the old and the new that remind
us of the bleeding practiced by medicine only a few centuries
ago. We are now firmly against the total practice of bleeding
as carried on then. But in one sense the fact is that modern
medicine has found superior ways of accomplishing the objective the old physicians had in mind when they bled a patient.
The disease was caused by a poison, they reasoned, and carried about by the blood. To get rid of the poison, get rid of
the blood. Modern medicine accepts the getting rid of the
poison. But it adds: to do so, either reinforce the natural agents
already combatting the poison, or neutralize the noxious agents.
The result—a penicillin injection, let us say, to prevent harm-
ful bacteria from reproducing—looks very different. It would
be possible to say that there is a difference of method. But the
methodological difference is far more than technique. It respects the natural powers fighting the disease, usually in the
bloodstream, as the old theory could not. Not only does it
work better; it has a firmer theory on which to rest. But it
has a similarity of objective even with the old and outworn
practice.

The analogy of new and old in pastoral counseling with
bleeding is quite inexact as to details. Our predecessors were
often wiser about the psyche than about the body. But the
general point of the metaphor seems relevant. The old is often
very good indeed; but even where its results are bad, there is
something positive in its intent. And the new, however novel,
is never so divorced from the tradition as at first appears.

COUNSELING, PSYCHOTHERAPY, AND
SOCIAL CASE WORK

At any time before the present century, one could have had
an utterly clear conscience in discussing pastoral help to people

while making nothing but the most casual references to other professional helpers. An appreciative nod to the old country doctor, and a reluctant commendation of the occasional family lawyer, would have taken care of this section. Most of the older books on pastoral theology and poimenics (Greek for the study of shepherding) did not even bother with that.

Our own age is very different. Psychiatrists, psychologists, and social workers are people of importance. Indeed, in view of the immense good that they accomplish, we pastors are in danger of being Johnny-come-latelies.

In the most violent brief in which we may put it, as Harry Stack Sullivan once asked, how is our pastoral counseling related to the psychotherapy of the psychiatrist and the clinical psychologist, and to the case work of the social worker?

One view of the answer is to see the pastor as a kind of first-aid worker. He sees that the injured man is not joggled, makes certain that his collar is open, applies smelling salts and cold handkerchiefs, and generally holds the fort until the doctor comes. There are times when one wishes this might be a true picture. But the trouble is that the doctor who finally comes, if he does, may know a good deal less about this particular kind of injury than the pastor does. And the notion that the clergyman is one without professional training in matters of counseling is increasingly wrong.

An opposite conception that has been heard of but rarely experienced is that the pastor is the sole specialist in these matters who really counts. So long as the sufferer does not need money or surgery, let the pastor take over. Psychiatrists are atheists and cannot be trusted; psychologists are nothing but testers; and social workers are all frustrated old maids. None of them know God. So let the pastor pray and bring religious resources. If people don't improve, it's because God has another plan for them. Of course all this is nonsense. But even though it appears infrequently, those few occasions should be nailed. It might be just as well to note the absolutely heretical theology involved in this position.

As always in Christian history, what the pastor and church actually do should depend in part upon ideal and in part upon practical considerations. It does not necessarily follow that the pastor is the ideal administrator of hydraulic devices because, in an emergency, the church at Rome ran the water supply in the fourth century. But even if we may say, ideally, that all serious psychoneuroses ought to be dealt with by a psychiatrist, it hardly follows that the pastor should gallop in the other direction the minute he smells a neurosis.

I am not at all prepared to admit that the pastor deals with superficial problems while the "deeper" problems are referred to other specialists. I know only too many competent and specially qualified pastors who can deal with psychotics, criminals, and others in great difficulty to be willing to suggest that such dealing is foreign to their pastorship. On the other hand, most pastors engage in a general rather than a special practice. For practical reasons of schedule, most can conduct only a limited number of counseling sessions with someone who needs help. In terms of hours spent with single individuals, the pastor cannot possibly be in the same class with the psychoanalyst. If he were, he would be neglecting several other important aspects of his work.

Part of the answer to this dilemma may be found by analyzing the conception of "depth" into its two principal components. As used in psychiatry and related disciplines, "depth" refers to factors of early origin and great psychic complexity, hence involving for therapeutic purposes extended time and highly technical skill. Except in emergencies, the pastor may be most grateful that others are now becoming available who may deal with problems of depth in this sense.

But depth has another meaning, in the sense of basic or ultimate significance. Depth in this sense must be a regular part of the pastor's concern. Such depth may appear in a first interview, just as it may in the ninety-ninth. What the pastor represents may evoke it. Depth in this sense is just as foreign to superficiality as is the depth which denotes complexity and early origin.

It is a very good thing, then, for the pastor to assume no responsibility beyond what he is plainly competent to handle. Like any truly professional person, he will make referrals not merely when he has reached his limit but also at any time another may be better prepared to give the needed help. But even if he refers, he still retains a pastoral obligation to the person. There is always a pastoral dimension even if the principal counseling is being done by a better qualified other. Those who keep warning pastors only of what they should not do have had little experience with real pastors. The pastors who take such warnings too seriously are those who could and should be doing more than they are doing. The imperialistic offenders never hear the warnings anyhow.

It is a most important discovery of psychiatry and the related modern disciplines that most problems that have emerged out of early origin and complex interactions require extended time for healing. Where this is the case, practical considerations prevent the pastor, even if technically qualified, from being the primary counselor. One way to put the matter is this. Draw a continuum line. Consider at one end the contemporary problems that may be dealt with contemporaneously. A teenager wants help in selecting a college. An open-minded convert wants information about the Presbyterians and Episcopalians so he may choose the lesser of two evils. Whatever the problem, the person is capable of viewing it as it is now, without undue hangovers from the past.

At the other end of the continuum put the problems that cannot even be faced because they are wholly clouded by unsolved problems of the past. This man wants a woman to love him, he thinks; but his desire cannot be met because he has failed to work through his mother attachment. That woman wants nothing so much as admiration; but the row of inconsequential medals she wears on her dress is a poor substitute. She will remain in a dead end until she can come to terms with that part of her remote past which has made her react against neglect and rejection in the direction of notice at any cost.

To the extent that the contemporary problem may be dealt with contemporaneously, relatively free from chains of the past, the pastor is clearly within his competence as well as his schedule. As he moves down the continuum toward the point where the present is nearly swallowed by chains from the past, both his schedule and his skill will be more dubious. He may, on occasion, have to act for pragmatic reasons, because no one else is available. And there are times when persons toward this end of the continuum will be responsive to a representative of the church when they would not to someone else. Depth in the sense of ultimacy is never foreign to the pastor. Of depth in the sense of complexity and early origin, he had best be wary unless he has the time and special training to follow through.

And what of the pastor's relationship to the social case worker, who is, in addition to being counselor, our greatest expert of all on relating particular personal problems to particular environmental resources? The trouble is that the social workers tend to be undervalued in this unique aspect of their function and competence. If a pastor has a family with a child who may be mentally deficient, and he seeks the counsel of the social worker on where to find out about this and what to do if it proves true, something very different is involved from calling "Information" for a number not listed in the telephone book. In his knowledge of environmental resources to help on personal problems, the pastor will be a general practitioner rather than a specialist. Here too, he may do much, but should know his limitations.

THE PASTORAL COUNSELOR

Every minister must be a pastoral counselor on occasion whether he wishes so or not. Even the most recondite theological scholar sometimes has his footnote work disturbed by a student who needs and wants something, knows it, and will remain until he glimpses the whites of the myopic professorial eyes. The one question is: good or bad?

It is always tempting, and never wholly wicked to present the character of the happy warrior, or the fully-functioning pastoral counselor. Ideally, he can be described as stable, mature, tolerant, understanding, appreciative, objective, concerned, dedicated, free, honest, conscientious, sensitive, cooperative, autonomous, etc. One is reminded of some of the recommendation forms that must be filled out, in which successive lines ask if the person is always cooperative in groups and always creative in action. Just how a person who is always creative in action could possibly be even tolerated in most groups is an open question. And precisely how the fully-functioning cooperator could have any time, let alone energy, left over for creativity is also elusive.

The fact, and the consolation, of the matter is that most pastoral counseling is done by pastors who are imperfect and by grace have some inkling of this state of affairs. We have no intention of giving aid and comfort to poor practice that could be remedied either by reasonable training or by a modicum of painful reflection on specific imperfections. But beyond all that, imperfection remains. And such imperfect pastors, conscious of their limitations, daily mediate enormous help. Their parishioners are helped by their skill, re-integrated by their concern, and re-directed by their clarification.

The problem, then, is not how to give ten years of post-graduate training to every pastor. It is partly a matter of giving enough training so that basic knowledge, wisdom, and skills are present. Of this we shall speak shortly. But it is also a matter of humility and the acknowledgment of ignorance where ignorance is a fact. Knowledge of ignorance is an immensely important form of knowledge, not least when it involves what one is not equipped to do. And if the humility is ever lost, even after ten years of special training, the counseling is likely to degenerate.

The wise preacher knows that, at best, his mediation of the truth of the gospel is translucent rather than transparent. He can never transcend an element of opaqueness. If he does not know this, he does not preach the gospel. If he does know it, then he may preach with that paradoxical confident humility that is so moving in practice and so hard to describe theoretically. So it is with the pastor as counselor. All the concentration in the world on desirable qualities like stability, sensitivity, or empathy will avail him nothing if he is unaware of his particular opaqueness to the communications of the other. But the recognition of this, far from being a barrier, proves to be like the gap over which the spark can jump. Some of the best results ensue when one is most conscious of his imperfections.

As inevitable pastoral counselors, let us by all means get some training. Let us do what we can to develop the right attitudes for counseling. But let us be alert to the work of the Holy Spirit which, while no cousin of obscurantists, nevertheless, often transcends our best intentions and redeems our worst actions.

EDUCATION FOR PASTORAL COUNSELING

Another aspect of this discussion is the story of clinical pastoral training, the uniquely American movement without which our talk of training for pastoral counseling would be a mere ontological gleam in some perceptive theologian's eye. What is really crucial about this training is the subjection of specific instances of one's own work to ruthless scrutiny by one's peers and seniors. Important though it has been to have such training in health and welfare institutions where people are in special need, to see underlying motives laid bare, to work under general supervision, and the like, the crucial educational values have always been *specific instances* and *ruthless scrutiny*.

As the clinical element has more and more been domesticated into the theological curriculum, progress has certainly been made at the fundamental point—its theological relevance—and the line of direction is clearer than it was. Yet the more we have succeeded in taming the clinical, the more it has become apparent that something else is needed as well. It seems to be a conviction of this kind, for instance, that began the Harvard program from which this volume has emerged.

Put rather schematically, the basic minimum education for pastoral counseling would look something like this. First, a good general education across the whole range of theological study, thought, and work: biblical, doctrinal, ethical, historical, etc. Without this the framework and context are either dim or offside. Second, some study of the clinical pastoral training type involving specific instances and ruthless scrutiny. Third, psychology in the general sense, examined from the points of view of pastoral practice and religious significance. Fourth, some pain-provoking reflection, enforced by such devices as term papers, on the relation of psychology and theology in pastoral counseling.

A good many theological schools have either achieved such a minimum, or are moving toward it. To extend such a "floor" program, and to move it optimally upward at least for some students, we are now clear that more far-reaching theoretical as well as practical work will be demanded. A few special scholars in the field must be made available. In this sense the work done by a few university-related theological schools is of great significance for all schools.

There should indeed be at least a certain basic minimum of training for pastoral counseling. And if this fails to include a clinical dimension, it runs counter to our best knowledge. But this may be of little avail unless it is set within a theological framework, and the potential encounter between theology and the personality sciences is carried out in fact—with all the uncertainties and ambiguities that are necessary and inevitable to such a genuine meeting.

PASTORAL COUNSELING IN THE MINISTRY

It is sometimes asked whether a preacher can possibly be a good pastoral counselor. As counselor, the questioner may say, one listens, attempts to understand, tries to get inside the other person's point of view, avoids condemnation or coercion, and helps to clarify. But as preacher, he adds, one must speak the truth even if it hurts, present the whole gospel and not merely its positive thinking dimension, chase out sin, interpret the cross realistically, and be a gadfly as well as a pillar. How, then, he may continue, can these two types of function be reconciled? Is the poor incumbent to have masks in his hip pocket, which he brings out for different occasions? And if he wears false faces, how is he ever to be integrated?

The trouble with this question lies not in what it says about pastoral counseling but in what it implies about preaching. And because of that error, it also misunderstands some things about counseling. Preaching is of course the attempt to witness to the whole gospel. But witness to whom? True preaching cannot possibly say anything to the congregation that is not also said to oneself. Preaching about the sinful, evil, suffering, and lost dimensions of our life as the gospel sees them is one thing if it reveals *our* predicament, but quite a different thing if it reveals *your* predicament from which either my collar or my character has automatically extricated me.

As a matter of fact, it is entirely unjustified to think that because counseling proceeds through acceptance and understanding it is devoid of the stern aspects of the gospel. When a parishioner is struggling painfully toward clarification, and we, suffering empathically with him, nevertheless realize that there is no substitute for this process, and hence avoid the so-called reassuring word that will have anything but a reassuring effect, we are actually engaging in acknowledgement of just those dark dimensions of life that are symbolized by the cross.

The other fact about Christian preaching is that it is in the indicative rather than the imperative mood. Granted that an "ought" or a "must" here and there may serve as rivets on the breastplate of righteousness, the basic function of preaching is showing the way things are—what is our problem and predicament as human beings, and what God has made available to us as answer and rescue. The ought of responsive action arises not out of exhortation, but out of conviction that both things *are* as they are—man's lostness, and God's salvation. Preaching declares that which, at the most basic level, *is*—the worst and the best.

Counseling too is in the indicative mood. We help a person to grasp what he really is—the best and the worst—knowing that this is far more powerful motivation for overall improvement than any prodding or encouragement to change himself. Thus in all the fundamental senses, and despite the obvious situational differences, the underlying kinship between counseling and preaching is very close. No false faces are required. If the preacher feels he needs a split personality in order to counsel, let him begin not by denigrating counseling but by re-examining his conception of Christian preaching. And incidentally, if the pastoral counselor depreciates preaching, let him think again and recognize that his every act and word and silence is a communication of some gospel or other, and he had best re-examine them to make sure his gospel is Christian.

Even if the minister is in a specialist's post, he must still communicate the gospel, organize the fellowship, and shepherd the sheep. Different pastors may perform these functions in different proportions. But no one escapes some responsibility for them all. Every pastor, then, we contend, must do some pastoral counseling. His one question is: will my work be effective or not?

In the growing conviction that pastoral counseling, as well as pastoral work in general, is inevitably a part of the ministry, and that therefore one had best know something about how to undertake it, there is immense promise of a greatly enriched ministry. This will help first those who meet all the conditions of counseling: admit they have a problem, locate part of it within themselves, seek help from the pastor, and assume some responsibility for the helping process. But it will help others besides, persons who are at some other point on the continuum that runs between resistance at one end to readiness for counseling at the other. There are many who are too lonely, bitter, alienated, anxious or guilty to admit they have a problem. If their smallest outreaches are met with understanding, their defenses will decline a minute fraction; and out of that may come the movement eventually making counseling possible. It is sobering to recognize that even our most casual contacts may hinder or further needed counseling. This makes it all the more important that we not profess one thing in a mythically isolated counseling to which we pay no heed on a pastoral call. With all our imperfections, we need to be the same person all through. A new assimilation of the importance of pastoral counseling, then, should imply a revitalization of our ministry as a whole; otherwise the pastoral counseling we have imbibed lacks a Christian body.

Pastoral counseling *is*, not ought to be, in the ministry. The question we must answer is: for good or for ill?

Theological Education after Ordination

REUEL HOWE

REUEL HOWE is the founder and first director of the Institute for Advanced Pastoral Studies in Bloomfield Hills, Michigan. Prior to this, he was Professor of Pastoral Theology at the Protestant Theological Seminary in Alexandria, Virginia. Beyond his training of parish ministers he has been well known for his effective speaking and discussion leadership in church groups. His book on *Man's Need and God's Action* contains his presentation of the Christian faith to modern man.

I. INTRODUCTION

A. *Natural limitations of pre-ordination training*

Studies of what happens to ministers after they are graduated from the seminaries, are ordained, and have served a few years in the ministry, raise some searching questions of theological education.

1. *Distinction between theological learning and training for the ministry*

First, how much longer can theological schools continue to be torn inconclusively between two often uncorrelated conceptions of their task: one which emphasizes almost exclusively a disciplined mastery of any one or all of the classical theological disciplines; and the other which stresses the preparation of students for the actual work of the ministry? The debate often waxes hot as to whether seminaries should be centers of theological learning or training schools for the ministry. When we accept that they are centers for theological learning, we may feel uneasy about our responsibility for preparing men for the work of the Church. When we accept their responsibility to train men for the ministry, we may feel that they are compromising their responsibility to preserve the faith through the discipline of scholarship. When seminaries try to do both, they feel overburdened. Furthermore, they find the correlation of the two emphases to be troublesome and difficult. *

We may agree on the theory that the correlation of theological learning and the work of the ministry is the responsibility of every member of the faculty, but all too often the two responsibilities are divided among faculty members with the result that a seminary may find itself operating with two competing programs, one representing the "practical" interests, and the other representing the classical academic ones. This creates a situation in which the student may feel that he must choose sides, as it were, which, if he does, produces in him a bias which will distort his ministry.

2. Difficulties in preparing men for an experience they have not had

A second question raised by a study of the results of theological education is: Can we accept that there is a natural limitation to how much we can accomplish in pre-ordination training? Many things stand in the way of preparing men for an experience they have not had. They have not borne the responsibilities of the ministry. They have not been challenged and confounded by the questions that people ask, nor by the ambiguities of the human situation. They have not known the prophet's loneliness, the pastor's bewilderment, and the teacher's sense of failure. Therefore, much that we may try to tell them about these experiences and the preparation we try to give them fall upon ears that cannot believe what they hear.

Students often turn from these unbelievable representations of what the ministry is like and find a false sense of security and competence in what appear to be the certainties of Biblical and doctrinal learning. These, they think, they know and understand; these have outlasted the ages; these, they think, will be effective when they tell people of them. Little do they realize, until several years after graduation, that their theological learning may have lured them away from an understanding of the people whom they went forth to teach and to serve, and increased the difficulties of communication between them and the world. More will be said about this kind of result of theological education later in the chapter.

Sufficient now is it to say that since theological education can cause such a separation of minister from people, no seminary faculty should allow itself to evade its responsibility to help the student correlate the answers of the Gospel and the questions of life. No seminary dare settle for being either a center of theological learning or merely a training school for the ministry. Every seminary needs to be both if its graduates are to be effective participants in the church's ministry in the world, whatever that ministry may be.

Every seminary faculty, however, needs to realize that no matter how much it improves its preparation of men for the ministry, there will always be this limit beyond which they cannot go, largely because students cannot ask some of the questions that open them to all the training they need for their work.

B. *Experiments toward improved training for the ministry*

However, we should try to improve the quality and effectiveness of theological education by a comprehensive and deep understanding of what is involved in the training of men for that work. In latter years curriculum additions and changes have been made in the interest of more relevant training for the ministry.

1. *Providing experiences like the ministry*

The addition of clinical pastoral training, supervised field work, and interne year programs have provided students with experiences that are like those of the ministry. These have been valuable additions to the preparation of ministers for their work, especially when they have been integrated into the theological curriculum and made a resource to every department as well as to the so-called practical departments. Some teachers of theology, for instance, are grateful for the kinds of questions that their students bring out of their clinical training and field work which give them an opportunity to show the relevance of Christian doctrines. At best, however, these resources provide students with only approximations of the kind of experiences that they will have after they have become ordained ministers. In the first place, they are not ordained when they take their clinical training or do their field work. In the second place, they do not have full pastoral responsibility for those to whom they minister. In the third place, they cannot possibly have a full experience of the ministry in any training situation to which they may be assigned. But these resources do provide the students with indispensable opportunities to live and work with people and to hear their questions. By these same means they discover how difficult it is to love people, and to help them, and they may begin to realize how important a resource for ministry is their relationship with people.

2. *The students' own experiences*

Then there are those experiments within the seminary itself that are designed to utilize the life experiences that the students bring to their training. They come to their studies with meanings, values, motives, and even a theology, with which they hear, respond to and resist all that their teachers try to impart. When the teacher recognizes this resource that the students possess, a change in the methods of theological education may take place. In general they change from what we may call the monological method to the dialogical one. The professor ceases to be a performer in which monologically he tells students what they ought to know. Instead, he becomes a prompter of a dialogue between the students and himself, the students and the people to whom they are to minister, and, implicitly, the students and God. The responsibility of the teacher is dynamically conceived in mutual relation to the responsibility of the learner. In this kind of teaching the content is less apt to become a barrier to the truths of which the content is supposed to be an expression. It is generally accepted among students of education that theological education has progressed less than any other branch of education. Seminary faculties, therefore, might study the processes by which learning occurs.

3. *The need of feed-back from graduates*

Then there are those experiments that are designed to produce for theological educators a feed-back from ministers whom they have prepared. A number of seminaries are calling back their graduates in order that they may test the effectiveness of the training given them. These schools have discovered that their graduates are asking questions that they had not been able to ask while they were in seminary with the result that they are now open to a training that was not possible then. Response to this observation is producing new developments in theological education and training for the ministry.

II. THE NEED FOR ADVANCED TRAINING

For years some seminaries have been holding workshops and refresher courses for their graduates and for others. Several denominations have been experimenting with in-service training programs of one sort or another. One of the most thorough studies of the possibilities of this type of training has been conducted by the Presbyterians during recent years.

A. *The Institute for Advanced Pastoral Studies*

Another new resource in post-ordination theological education has been the establishment of the Institute for Advanced Pastoral Studies in Bloomfield Hills, Michigan, of which the author of this chapter is the director. The Institute, while designed to explore the possibilities of post-ordination training for Protestant ministers, has uncovered also significant information about the needs of clergy.

Before the ministers attend an Institute session, they fill out a questionnaire designed to draw from them their interests and needs. From the returned questionnaires, the agenda for each session is constructed. A typical agenda for a ten-day conference, indicating areas of concern felt generally by the clergy, follows:

A TYPICAL AGENDA

I. What is the Church? Its Purpose?

    A. As institution and as servant of the Spirit

    B. The Church's ministry: Purpose?
       Clericalism vs. Church as Laos

    C. Self-centered Church vs. Church as Mission
       Relation of Church to modern industrial society

II. The Minister as Pastor

    A. Pastoral counseling

       Purpose of counseling
       Principles of counseling
       Resources for counseling

B. Relation between pastoral work and preaching
   The dialogical character of Christian preaching

C. Correlations between pastoral work and theology

III. The Minister as Bearer of the Gospel:
   Communication

   A. Communication to people today

      1. How can the Good News be communicated to people for whom Biblical symbols and myths are strange?

      2. How can the truth of the Gospel be communicated with power and relevance?

      3. How can we help laymen become more responsible and intelligent about Christian faith?

      4. How can real communication and mutual understanding be achieved between laymen and clergymen?

   B. Christian education

      1. What is the basic purpose of the Church's teaching ministry?

      2. With children and adults, how can the tension between concern for the subject matter and concern for persons be understood and managed?

      3. What are the purposes in training teachers and leaders?

      4. What are the dynamics of group life? What is the function of the leader?

IV. The Minister as a Leader of the People of God:
   Administration and Organization

   A. What realistic possibilities are there for organizing time for important ministries, study, and family?

   B. How can the heavy load of administrative details best
      be managed?

   C. By what standards shall the Church plan and evaluate
      its ministry? Its meetings and services?

   D. Training lay leaders: How can we best minister to
      and with laymen?

V. The Minister as a Person

   A. Conflicts between personal and professional life of
      minister

   B. How can we live and work with personal inadequa-
      cies?

   C. What resources are there for ordering one's devo-
      tional life and functional efficiency?

Both the questionnaires and the conferences reveal needs
that raise questions about theological education generally and
training for the ministry specifically.

B. *What happens to seminary graduates in the ministry?*

One wonders why theological educators are not more curi-
ous about the results of the training they give their students
rather than assuming, as is so easy to do, that their teaching
adequately prepares their graduates for their ministries. Con-
tinuingly and probingly we should ask such questions as these:
What happens to ministers after they have completed their
theological education? Did their training help them face the
parish problems? How far were they unprepared? In what
ways did they develop resources on their own to deal constructively with the pastoral problems which arise? How effectively are they able to bring the meanings of the Gospel into
redeeming dialogue with the meanings of modern man? An-

swers to these questions are available if we will give ministers opportunity, under supervision, to evaluate the meaning of their training in terms of satisfactions and problems experienced in their work. And the securing of answers to these questions is one of the purposes of post-ordination training programs, especially those in which the theological educator and the minister are willing to engage in honest dialogue. This kind of dialogue engaged in at the Institute for Advanced Pastoral Studies has produced some answers that are worthy of attention.

Before citing the following answers, it should be made clear that the ministers who have attended the Institute and whose statements we have recorded here, are from eleven denominations, studied at more than forty seminaries including all the major ones, both denominational and non-denominational, and were invited because of their qualifications, experience, and interest in further preparation for their ministry. The foregoing needs to be said lest the reader attribute some of the comments to malcontents and misfits.

1. *Satisfactions experienced in the ministry*

It is not surprising, and should be first of all affirmed, that many ministers have real experiences of satisfaction in their work. Of the five ministerial functions: preaching, pastoral care, teaching, priestly and organizational or administrative responsibilities, it is clear that preaching and pastoral functions are the sources of the greatest satisfaction. The ministers from the more liturgical churches seem to value their pastoral relationship above every other, and the ministers from the free churches seem to value the preaching function above every other. Teaching seems to be third choice in both cases, with the priestly responsibilities coming next, and the administrative and organizational work being the source of least satisfaction for most ministers. Most of them, however, are frustrated because they have to spend much more time in administrative and organizational work than they do in any other. And many of them complain that they were not trained for this work and do not feel adequate in the management of the church's institutional life.

Examining their satisfactions a little more closely we find that they rejoice in being able to help people in times of trouble, the "privilege of sharing people's burdens and helping them find and hold fast to the Gospel." They appreciate "having a part in the significant experiences of their people such as baptisms, funerals, marriages."

Many find satisfaction in participating in the changes in peoples' lives. They cite the joy they feel in "seeing the developing faith of their people and in participating in their growth," in "leading people to new allegiance with Christ and the Church." They appreciate a "congregation which has grown in purpose and responsibility," or responding to "questions that indicate interest in the Christian life and in the Church," or ministering to "teen-agers as they mature and begin to make significant life decisions."

Another area in which they find much satisfaction is in communication and especially in preaching. Their special delight is in being able to preach sermons that meet the needs of people. However, many report that this seems to happen only occasionally, and they wish they could do so more often. They speak of "getting through only occasionally," or "I am always looking for new ways of relating the Gospel to bewildering human problems." Others, speaking of the satisfaction to be found in preaching and in teaching, express the wish that they might find ways in which they could determine how effective their preaching really was.

Their relationship to laymen is another area in which satisfaction is experienced. Although there is much evidence on the part of ministers that they sense a barrier between them and their lay people, and that the "chasm of communication is very wide," still when a "real meeting" takes place there is enthusiastic appreciation for a creative relationship with laymen. They rejoice in "laymen who can articulate their convictions." Many are most appreciative of "the warmth and responsiveness of their people." They delight in the fellowship of "my people and the joy of being with them." There is praise of "people's dedication and faith, often in the face of adversity." Satisfaction is also expressed in the growth of the institutional church with its expanding program and a feeling of joy in "my role and the direction of parish work."

2. Problems of ministers

While these are the areas of satisfaction for many ministers, they are also the sources of frustration, irritation, and bewilderment.

a. Images of the ministry

Many problems of the clergy seem to center around the image they have of themselves and the image their people have of them. An image is a picture or concept which describes a stereotype of a person or group. They are acquired from others, and may be false and misleading. We feel that we have to fit these stereotypes and are not free to be ourselves.

There are two sets of images at work in the life of the Church. First, there are the minister's images: of himself as a minister, for example someone who always must have the right answer; of himself as a person, for example one who is always wrong; and of his people, both individually and congregationally, as his judges. All this is set in the context of his image of the Church, its teachings, and its various relationships.

Second, there are the congregation's images: of themselves as a congregation, for example a group of choice people; and of the minister, what he represents and what they should expect of him, such as the man on the pedestal. Beneath these images live both the minister and the congregation as they really are, realities which may never consciously meet because their respective images keep them both acting out roles with each other. Since our images of ourselves influence our goals and behavior, it should come as no surprise that ministers are lost in confusion about themselves, their family, congregational and community relations, and their job! And, of course, there are the images which obstruct and confuse communication between the Church and the world.

Many ministers admit they do not feel free as ministers to be themselves, or, as one man put it, free to "be my own kind of minister." The influences of other ministers, teachers, and concepts of the minister are planted in them from their youth and imprison them. The effects of movie portrayals of the minister are strong and destructive. An able, devoted minister said, "I am glad to be a minister, and I hate being one, too, because as a minister, I am forced to be less than I am as a person." Another able man claimed that accepting himself as a minister was difficult for him. Many of them feel that they are put on a pedestal which, as one said, "is wrong because there is not room on it for anyone else, especially for my people in the midst of whose lives I ought to live." They dislike the "pedestal" role forced upon them. Yet they need, as another said "to have my people think better of me than they ought to think." One man was afraid to play with his son in the front yard for fear that his people would think that he did not have anything better to do.

Many ministers are anxious about this problem because they do not know how to deal with it. Their anxieties carry over into uncertainties about their role: "I do not know whether I should take the initiative in trying to help in situations where trouble is developing and tragedy is certain." And there are the uncertainties as to what to communicate and how: "What is the relevance of the Gospel to human problems?" "How can we effectively relate people to Christ?" "Should a parish priest be a pastoral counselor?" "Does the parish minister have a prophetic role in the community?"

b. *The ministers' inadequacies*

Then, there are their professional inadequacies such as "my pastoral opportunities are mostly one-shot affairs." "What is wrong with my efforts to establish rapport with my people?" "I am a lousy teacher. I speak with an uncertain voice. People do not come back for more." "I do not know how to relate the theology that I learned in seminary to the people to whom I minister and their problems." "I am uncertain about my own capacity to deal with people's problems and their underlying feelings. I get involved with them and cannot be an instrument of God's grace." There are many statements that indicate inadequacy in counseling, in study and prayer life, in sermon preparation and discipline, in being able to give adequate attention to pastoral cases; ignorance in counseling couples nearing divorce, in ministering to the bereaved; inability to communicate with young people and adults; fear of children and fear of lay people. Considerable uncertainty and self-consciousness in preaching are expressed. "The image of great preachers that I acquired in Seminary intimidates me and stands in the way of my own preaching." Many ministers feel that in spite of their efforts their messages are not heard. They do not know how to communicate to modern man. "The language of the Bible and of traditional Christian theology is not heard by contemporary man, and I do not know how to speak the Gospel to him in terms in which he can understand and accept it." Or, "I enjoy teaching, but I am not happy about the results."

Many ministers hold expectations that are not being fulfilled, and are consequently bewildered by lack of results from their efforts. Many of them expected that as ministers they would have an opportunity to lead the Church in a courageous Christian facing of great social issues. Instead they find that church people are cautious, conservative, fence-sitters, and unwilling to commit themselves in controversial matters. Many of these clergy are criticized by their people for taking stands in social issues and for even preaching sermons that apply to them. As indicated earlier, many of them are appalled at the lack of response or of significant response to sermons. They had expected that the exercise of their ministry would produce radical transformations in individual and social life which they do not see. Conversions seem few, and they do not know how to reach the indifferent. They are often dismayed that their services as a minister are not sought out by their people in times of sickness, death, and other crises, and they do not know what to do about these problems.

Their relationships with their laymen cause them considerable concern. They feel that their teaching and preaching is not understood and that they do not know how to communicate meaningfully. They find it difficult to help laymen apply Christian principles in their daily life and to arouse interest in the Christian faith. On the other hand, these same ministers often show a singular lack of understanding of the nature and meaning of the work that laymen are doing in the world, and fail to see it as the point at which the Gospel might engage in dialogue with the world. Because the ministers do not see laymen's work as ministry, they cannot very well help the laymen recognize it as such, with the result that both ministers and laymen tend to regard as Church work only the services rendered the Church organization. Ministers feel that they are being caught up more and more into the demands of the institutional Church, and are less and less able to practice the ministry of the redemptive community for which they entered the Lord's service.

Problems of authority also contribute to feelings of professional inadequacy. Many feel that they have no authority as ministers; others are embarrassed by the authority they bear and do not know how to exercise it. Still others, however, and large numbers are included here, give and expect rigid obedience to a false or idolatrous kind of authority such as obedience to the authority of ordination per se, to doctrinal systems and propositions, to liturgical usages, to scriptural literalism, or, strangely, to psychological relativism. All of these are ways by which ministers seek to justify their ministry and by which they reveal how insecure they are in their historic role.

There are the personal inadequacies of the ministers also. Many of them are restless and uncertain about their vocations. A surprising number of them, because of the disappointment in the ministry, have been and are considering the possibility of resigning and taking up other work. Men, who sought ordination because they could not find a ministry as laymen, are now thinking of resigning the ministry and returning to the work of laymen in order to find their ministry.

A common source of unrest is an impatience with people and an inability to accept them as they are. It is surprising how many ministers enter their work with illusions about themselves and people. They often confess to being surprised at the shallowness of their love for others, and are dismayed to discover that far from loving people, they may positively dislike them. The dislike is largely due to their inability to understand human behavior, to recognize its motivation, and to accept the purposes that lie behind the symptoms they dislike; therefore, they are unable to minister deeply to their people.

Their frustrations in the ministry, of course, raise questions about their faith because it is shaken. It is disquieting for them to discover that what they thought was their faith is only as strong as their ability to do the work for which they have not been prepared.

A majority of the men confess to undisciplined living and to lack of ability to organize their time and achieve a structure for their work. They recognize, of course, that because of the nature of the ministry and the unexpected emergencies of life which are the source of demands upon them, it is naturally difficult to achieve a disciplined way of life. Many of them are demoralized by these demands and live from moment to moment, responding to that which exerts the most immediate and strongest pressure. The result is that their living, by their own admission, is haphazard and frazzled. The effect of this upon the family life of the clergy is not hard to imagine. The tensions between the demands of the ministry and the desire for family life are tremendous. Most of them feel guilty about their responsibilities to wife and children, and there is very real evidence of tragedy in the homes of many of our ministers.

c. *The problem of irrelevance*

One of the main concerns of the clergy is for theological relevance. They long to proclaim the Gospel to their people so that they will hear its saving meaning, but at this point they are frustrated and discouraged. They speak, but their people do not hear, with the result that the clergy begin to wonder about the power of the Christian faith, the efficacy of the sacraments, and the symbols given to them for the communication of the Gospel. They are baffled because in spite of their best efforts in preaching and teaching, their people still think that Christianity is a do-it-yourself religion: that one is saved by keeping the Commandments, following the teachings of Christ, and obeying the Golden Rule.

It is to be hoped, if not assumed, that seminary teachers did not intend their graduates to use the language of the seminary in their communications with their people. Yet this is exactly the language that most ministers seem to use. The result has been that much theological training of ministers has educated men away from the possibility of communication with their people. They, themselves, claim that they are less able to speak to them with meaning than they were before they received their training. Much of their understanding of Christianity is dated understanding which means they think about its meanings in terms of past ages and cultures. They find it easy to begin a sermon on a passage from the Letters to the Corinthians by trying to get their congregations to pretend they are Corinthians. They find themselves more at home with the relevance of the Gospel for other times, places, and people. Their preoccupation with the past stifles their power of communication with people today, especially since the ability to transpose historical insights from one age to another seems to be lacking.

This means that they cannot recognize and engage in the dialogue between the meanings of the Gospel and the meanings of peoples' lives. They admit that their theological interpretations are monological and are couched in the same language as their textbooks. There, if it lives at all, the Gospel rests, an alien and inert deposit in the minds and hearts of their people. The ministers were given a theology to be delivered propositionally, not a theology for encounter, and so lack the capacity to understand theologically the thought and behavior of their people, or to recognize in this thought and behavior the questions that require a new approach.

They find it difficult to engage in theological thinking, partly because of their fear of heresy. They tend to cleave closely to systematic doctrinal thinking, and are unable to explore courageously the meanings of the Gospel as they are focused on the different areas of human life. This makes for sterility, causing them to place an excessive value on the forms of theological thought, and making them defensive about the Faith. On the other hand, since they acknowledge that the Faith has the power of God behind it, they do not understand why they should be so afraid of the unorthodox. It comes as a relief to them, therefore, to discover that heresy can be a sign of a thinking Church and that exclusive orthodoxy can be a sign that the Church is intellectually asleep. They are quick to admit that the times seem to call for creative and courageous dialogue between the Gospel and the world, rather than a rigid application of propositions about Christian truth.

The clergy want to think about theology in relation to life and use the theological insights, but many of them have never received training for this. For example, they can preach excellent sermons on the subject of justification by Faith, but they do not as easily perceive that the modern status-seeking man, who by his status-seeking is trying to justify himself, needs fully to understand the meaning of this doctrine.

d. *The problem of communication*

The preceding illustration also raises the question of communication. The common conception is that it consists of telling people what you want them to know. The ministers explain that the conception is acquired from their seminary teachers. This is not surprising, especially when one realizes, as Dr. Samuel Blizzard has reported in his study of seminary graduates, that the most influential mentor image for ministers is usually one or more of their seminary professors. Certainly many clergy report that they think of themselves carrying out the picture of him lecturing to the class out of the wonderful things that he knows and believes. Young ministers proceed to follow this example, only to discover with dismay that their congregations do not accept their "lecture" the way they think the seminary lectures were accepted and assimilated.

It should be pointed out here that the author of this chapter in no way belittles the importance of the lecture method of teaching. But anyone who has made any kind of a serious study of how people learn knows that the lecture is only one tool among many, and is meant to be used with other tools. An exclusive use of it fails to educate. This is the experience of thousands of ministers. Their assumption that if they tell people the truth, they will hear it, has been blasted. That the "one-way street" concept of communication is inadequate to the task of preaching the Gospel today is the report of most ministers who are thoughtful enough to observe the results of their preaching and teaching and who are honest enough to admit it.

Furthermore, few of them report that they are using any dependable means by which they can check on the results of their communication. Sermons are preached, and instructions are given with the assumption that if they know their subject and present it in an organized and clear way, it will have the desired effect. Instead, many of them are appalled to discover how little their people do understand, and how greatly what they have said has been misinterpreted and misrepresented unintentionally.

e. *Doctrinal inadequacy for the ministry*

Many ministers suffer from a doctrinal inadequacy for their ministry in that they do not base their Christian life and work on the work of the Holy Spirit. They are caught up in and worn out by the tensions between the Church as Institution and the Church as Mission. They would like to engage more in the Church's mission to the world, but instead they feel that they are mainly called upon to be the director of an organization that is concerned more about its own competitive survival than in its redemptive purpose. They feel that they are personally responsible for the work of the Church, that its success or failure depends upon them, and that they alone have its important work to do. They resent being cut off by their office from normal association with other men, and yet they increase their separation by clerical pre-occupations. From these conditions result the twin diseases of the Church, namely, the clericalism that blocks the ministry of the laity and limits the ministry of the clergy, and parochialism which is the Church's chief symptom of its pre-occupation with itself.

Conspicuously absent or distorted in the ministers' concept of their role is the Holy Spirit Who created the Church in the first place and Whose work is the completion of Christ's work among men. If they think of Him at all, they think of the Holy Spirit as one Who will help them rather than their being participants in His work. Their theological training did not make clear to them how completely dependent they are upon the Holy Spirit for living the Christian life as well as for carrying on a Christian ministry. Many of them are anxious, defensive, fragmented, competitive, and jealous of their own prerogatives. The same lack of dependence upon the Spirit for guidance lays them wide open to denominational competition, pre-occupation with the importance of Orders, and other things that continue to divide the Church.

f. The agenda anxiety

One of the most obsessive anxieties suffered by the clergy is what we may call agenda anxiety, which is another sign of a lack of faith in the presence and work of the Spirit. They are so concerned about getting the content of the Christian Faith across to their people that they become oblivious to, and fail to reach, the people for whom it was given. For instance, they try to prepare young couples for marriage by presenting them with the theory of Christian marriage; and, if they do not succeed in covering the subject, they are afraid they have failed. Many clergy confess, however, that even their most organized lectures often fail to give the help needed. Their discourses more often meet their own need to teach rather than their people's need for help. These people are not yet ready to relate to the content and to accept it.

Most of the clergy who come to the Institute for advanced study are still victims of content illusion. This will continue to be the case as long as seminaries continue to teach subject matter exclusively and, in so doing, overlook their responsibility for the student. A man filled with subject matter does not make an adequate minister. An adequate minister must be a man in whom the meanings of life and the meanings of the Gospel are being correlated. The "didactic and dogmatic stance" referred to by Richard Niebuhr in his "Advancement of Theological Education" produces a ministry that is unequal to proclaiming the Gospel in this time when profound questions are being asked in every aspect of life. Ministers trained in this way come to resent the indignity of having been turned into subject-matter midgets instead of ambassadors for Christ.

III. RECOMMENDATIONS FOR
THEOLOGICAL EDUCATION

I wish now to make some recommendations for theological education that grow out of our experience with ministers who have been engaged in their ministry for at least three years. The first set of recommendations is for theological seminaries and is concerned with pre-ordination training. The second set of recommendations concerns post-ordination, or advanced, training that is being given, or might be given, to seminary graduates after a period of time in the ministry.

A. *For pre-ordination training*

The training of men for the Christian ministry is a profoundly important task. Upon it depends the training of the Church's leadership, both clerical and lay, because clergy in turn become the trainers of the laity. The influence of theological schools, therefore, is incalculable for good or ill, depending upon the kind of preparation they give. If the religious and theological subject matter is treated as an end in itself, the leadership of ministers will tend to be irrelevant and ineffective. If a monological concept of preaching and teaching is given to ministers by their training, they will not know how to lead the Church in a dialogical engagement with the world with the result that the Church will not understand the world and the world will not hear the Church's proclamation of the Good News. To a terrifying degree, the accomplishment of the Church's mission depends upon theological education in the work in which the seminary teacher is a profoundly important person!

The first recommendation for pre-ordination training calls for a rethinking of the role of the seminary teacher. Seminary personnel should be held up to the comparable rigorous standards of originality, productivity, and effectiveness of workers in other fields. One of the first questions to be asked is: How can seminary teachers be most effectively employed as regards their training, talents, and departmental responsibilities? Once this question is asked we are immediately confronted by the prevailing stereotype of the seminary professor, who, because he knows or employs only one pedagogical tool, the lecture, passes on to successive generations of students his stereotyped pattern of communication; or, even worse, fails to educate them.

The lecture is not only an ancient, but also an honorable and effective method of teaching. It gives the great teacher opportunity to impart through the genius of his personality the liberating power of truth; and, in so doing, to inform, guide and inspire his students. But let us also admit that it gives the pedant opportunity to becloud the truth and to bore his students.

The purpose of the lecture is to illumine, inspire, and awaken the learner to commitment, and, as such, is one of the indispensable tools of education. But it is only one of the tools; and if used exclusively, is as inadequate to the whole task of education as would be a carpenter's exclusive use of the hammer in building a house. Furthermore, much lecturing, according to reports of students, duplicates material already available in assigned textbooks. In earlier times when books were not as available, lectures were needed in order that students might acquire the necessary content for their education. Now, however, the lecture method should be used to meet other needs.

Individual teachers and the entire faculty as a team should examine how best they can use their personal and technical equipment in the accomplishment of their purpose. Honest teachers admit that they need help to keep from drifting into the role of performers with their classes as their audiences. Rather, teachers are needed as resource persons, knowledgeable and wise, who seek to help students correlate human questions and the Gospel. The responsibility of true teachers is not just to give students answers. Who would be better qualified, by virtue of what they know and understand, than the teachers that help students ask the great questions thus preparing them, as otherwise they cannot be prepared, for significant learning? Who better able to direct their reading and thinking, and who more tragically irresponsible if they do the students' work for them? Teachers who use their powers to help students find their own powers, because they know their pupils and know where they are in their studies and preparation, may lecture when it is appropriate to do so, as a part of a dialogue in which their students are significant participants. In the context of this kind of learning students will hear the lecture and be moved and changed by its meaning.

Mention was made earlier of the faculty as a team. Some faculties resemble a chorus of prima donnas all singing from a different score. Is it too utopian to hope that faculty members might seek to accomplish their task by a complementary employment of themselves, their responsibilities, and their methods? Theological education becomes more effective when the theological curriculum is de-departmentalized, at least to the point where communication occurs across departmental boundaries. The competitive emphasis on the mastery of any or all parts of the theological subject matter as an end in itself fragments the future ministers' understanding of the living form of the Gospel, and shakes his belief in its power to engage the world in meaningful dialogue.

Training for the ministry would be more helpful if it could also be made less abstract and theoretical. Theory is indispensable to thought and action, but the expounding of theory apart from the problem to which it belongs is irresponsible. Of course, it is easier to theorize about justification by faith, for example, then it is to present the truth of that doctrine in dialogue with the students' recognition of their own and other people's attempts at self-justification. The employment of the case method of teaching would help us to restore the dialogue between theory and practice, and would be compatible with

the Biblical concept of truth as action. The pastoral department could provide the situation in which students would experience and recognize the question and the need of justification, and the way people try to meet it. The study of the
Bible and History would show the self-justifying struggles of
man, and the action of God through the Prophets, Christ and
the Church. The study of theology in its various branches
would bring the human question of the need of justification
into focus and reveal its deeper meaning: if, for example,
status-seeking were seen as self-justification, it would open the
person to the possibility of accepting the meaning of justification by faith. The various disciplines of preaching, teaching,
pastoral care, and priestly direction would address themselves
to the task of effective communication of God's answer to the
question of what man needs. A drama of learning would be
created in which content, meaning, and relationship would
combine into what could be amazingly effective preparation
for the ministry.

Finally, students should be given more of the basic and
seminal books to read in order to become familiar with the
most creative and profound Biblical and theological thinkers;
assignments should make a contribution to the dialogue rather
than be a substitute for thinking. There is very little point in
education that does not educate, and teaching that does not
make the pupil a master of disciplined study. But the pupil
cannot master theological learning unless he is able to employ
it in relation to its natural object, namely, that part of life
which raises the questions that bring out its relevance.

Students need to experience this kind of instruction as an
example to emulate. Especially is this so since it has been
demonstrated that seminary teachers have such a formative
influence on their students. They would be greatly helped if,
day after day, they could see their teacher's masterful direc-

tion of the learning process, have him evoke the questions that bring them into active dialogue with the great thinkers of all ages, experience the patience with which he allows them to do their own creative thinking, and yet feel his guidance as they thread their way to authentic knowledge and insight. This experience of learning in relation to the teacher as one having authority would produce ministers who, in their turn, would teach, preach, and minister as men having true authority.

Seminaries, especially denominational ones, might consider how they may more adequately prepare their graduates for an ecumenical ministry. While the world organizes itself for interplanetary exploration and existence, it is ridiculous for the Christian Church to remain so helplessly split into divisions that are more symbolic of the quarrelsomeness of human nature than of the unity that Jesus Christ was supposed to have achieved for men. The world, which is struggling with its own problems of political and economic unity and peace, needs Christian ministers who can provide spiritual leadership for the task, statesmen who transcend denominational competition and controversy and bring perspective to men's thoughts about their problems. Denominationalism will become as obsolete as nationalism, and seminaries might try to make a powerful contribution to its obsolescence.

B. *Graduate image reconsidered*

A reconsideration of the graduate image for seminary students is also in order. As we have seen, one of the chief sources of difficulty for the modern minister is his image of himself as a minister and the relation of himself as a person to that image. A study of the experiences of men in the ministry indicates two outstanding and desirable characteristics of the image toward which theological education might be directed.

1. *Minister as coach or prompter*

The first characteristic of the image is of the minister as a coach or prompter rather than as a one-man team. The one-man team concept of the ministry has proved inadequate. Considering the tremendous opportunity the Church has to-day, the shortage of clergy poses a distressing problem. There is no solving it in the foreseeable future, if we continue on our present assumption that the professional ministry constitutes the whole ministry of the Church. To reach men significantly with the Gospel in our times we must increase the ministry a hundredfold, and the only way of doing that is to return to the great Biblical doctrine of the priesthood of all believers and affirm again that all Christian men and women are servants and ministers of Christ and His Church. If the whole ministry of the Church were to be activated for the Church's mission to the world, the role of the clergy would have to be different. The major part of his responsibility would be to train and direct the work of the laymen as they witness to Christ in that part of the world in which they live. Instead, a great deal of seminary education contributes directly to the concept of the clerical nature of the ministry of the Church. And too many attempts to activate the lay ministry tends to make them assistants to the clergy. More daringly we should view the clergy as the assistants to and the guides of the ministry of the laymen: the servants of the servants.

If the minister is to be a coach or prompter, some preconditions for this role will have to be realized. First, it is imperative that he know deeply what it means to be a person living the human life with other persons. This cannot be taken for granted. It does not follow that because a man has lived for twenty or forty years he knows what it means to be a person, or that he brings such knowledge to his theological training. It is the responsibility of the seminary to teach him to know himself as a person living in relation to others, by means of such resources as clinical training, field work, interne programs, psychotherapy, and the aims of his study and worship life in the seminary community. Often there is a lack of correlation between the man and his office. If a man goes into the ministry as a way of evading the real questions of his human existence, he cannot be a true minister.

Second, he needs to recognize himself as a member of the laos—the people of God. Too many ministers, it seems, bypass this identity and find their meaning as ordained ministers. Ordination thus becomes another means of self-justification. Unless the priesthood or ministry is grounded in this concept of the whole people of God, the development of clericalism and hierarchical conceptions of the ministry will inevitably develop. These are inimical to the truth of the fellowship of the Holy Spirit.

Third, men in their original training for the ministry need help in recognizing and accepting their dependence upon the Holy Spirit for carrying on the work of the ministry. The Church is the incarnation of the Holy Spirit and all the people of God, ordained or not, are the instruments of the Spirit. This concept stands in sharp contrast to the practice of many ministers who most of the time rely upon themselves and who only remember the Holy Spirit as a resource for helping them out of a difficulty. The right understanding of the Church's ministry as dependent on the Spirit would radically change the ministers' view of their own task and that of the laity. Furthermore, they would have a basis for accepting the tension between vitality and form, between the Spirit and the various forms that develop in the life of the Church and often threaten to strangle it. The leadership of the Church would be much more creative if they could be freed from slavery to obsolete form and open to the Spirit's guidance in the creation of new ones. Church life reveals the need for greater expectation and acceptance of the unusual and extraordinary as opposed to the normal and mediocre.

Fourth, seminary students need help in recognizing that the Church's mission is to the world and not to the Church. There is too much preoccupation with the Church as an institution and not enough with its responsibilities to the world in which it is set. Along with and even as part of the study of the Bible, the history of the Church, theology, and pastoral care, should go the study of the world in which the Church now lives and in which its ministry will have to be carried on. More needs to be done to familiarize students with the cultural influences that are dynamically opposed to the working of the Spirit. They need to recognize those parts of the secular life that can be affirmed in relation to those parts which need to be brought under judgment. They need to understand the values that men find in their work, and to be able to show them how this work of serving the world may be offered to God as worship. Only by participating in the Church's true dialogue with the world can the clergy help people to understand what they are accepting when they accept the Christian Faith or what they are rejecting when they reject it. It is not that ministers do not know their theology, but that they do not understand the meaning of life, and the relation of theology to life. Many of them, therefore, are bitter because they feel they are dealing with the trivial aspects of life and religion, rather than with the depth of meaning in the encounter between the Church and the world.

Finally, seminaries could help their students see the unity that binds the different functions of the ministry. It is ridiculous for ministers to choose between being priests as against being preachers or pastors, or choose being pastors as against being teachers and administrators, as if such a division of the dynamically interrelated Christian ministry were possible. There is too much equating of the work and fruits of the Spirit with the human talents of men. God may use a man's talents or He may seem to ignore them and call him to a work for which he does not have a natural talent. Here again the applied doctrine of the Holy Spirit is essential. We do not enter the ministry on the basis of our talent alone. We enter because we are called by One Who is doing His work in the world and Who will use those who surrender themselves to Him. But because He is the worker there is a unity in the different functions that we perform. When we teach we are also caring for souls, and our pastoral care gives opportunity also to teach. The principles of teaching are equally relevant to counseling and preaching. The interrelationships of the different functions of the ministry derive from the unity of God's working, and from the basic principles of relationship upon which all functions of persons and, therefore, of the ministers, must depend. A sense of this unity of the ministry is needed by ministers not only for the sake of their work but also for the sake of their health as workmen.

2. Minister as dialogist

The second characteristic of the new image of graduate ministers is that they be dialogists rather than monologists. In this respect they have two responsibilities. Their first responsibility is for the meaning people bring to hearing and learning. If theological students have not become aware of this responsibility before arriving at the seminary, they certainly should learn it while there. And there would be no better way for them to learn it than by having their teachers make them aware of the meanings they bring to their own theological education, on the basis of which they will make their responses.

The meanings which they bring to the educational encounter explain their understandings and misunderstandings. Theological professors would be less mystified at the lack of results from their teachings if they could see and understand that the results are not entirely dependent upon their efforts but also upon the influence of the meanings and beliefs that students bring to their training. Since this is the case, it would be wise for them, as well as for all teachers, to give their students an opportunity to speak and act out of what they bring. The usual objection to this procedure is that teachers, who may also be learned men, do not like to have pupils speak out of their ignorance; but a little more tolerance on the teachers' part for this ignorance and ineptness as a part of learning might increase their effectiveness. Unless attention is paid to what men bring to their training and opportunity is given them to enter into honest dialogue with their teachers, whatever "education" they otherwise might receive will be like a veneer laid over the real attitudes, values, and beliefs by which they live. One minister eloquently testified that he was in possession of two theologies, the "classical" one that he acquired at the seminary and the "bastard" one that he had developed during his life and which had continued to grow even after he had graduated from seminary. The latter was a more dynamic one and unconsciously influenced his ministry. The other was the one he employed from the pulpit and platform. He observed that both he and his people were puzzled by the contradictions between the two "systems." The point of the present recommendation is, therefore, that seminaries should assume more responsibility for the meanings that men bring with them out of their life and thought and provide them with opportunities for illumining and transforming dialogue.

Students who go through this kind of process themselves will be trained to do the same thing in relation to their people.

Having been helped to ask their own questions and thus prepared to hear the Gospel, they will be better able to help their own people to ask questions in order that they, too, may be prepared to hear and receive the Gospel. They will want to help their people to understand the meaning of their own experiences and see the theology implicit in them, and, therefore, to see their need for the affirmation and correction of Christian belief. Ministers' attitudes toward human behavior might then be different. Instead of seeing it as something to either approve or reject, they will recognize it as a kind of a sign language that will tell them something about people, to whom they will now be able to minister with understanding.

The second responsibility of the ministers who are dialogists is to teach and preach the Gospel in relation to these understandings and meanings that people bring to their encounter with the Gospel. Their ministry will be life-centered rather than agenda-centered. They will be willing to hold the interests of subject matter and the concerns of people in creative tension, and will fight any premature resolution of the tension by settling either for subject matter or persons. Such ministers will be able to know what they believe and their beliefs will inform their work. There their techniques of preaching, teaching, and pastoral care will be the instruments of their Faith rather than substitutes for it. We need pastors who can think theologically and theologians who can think pastorally. We may understand the dialogical character of theological education when we recognize that it may be both the agent of the faith which is God's grasping the students through the action of their teachers and others, and the awakener in them of a faith which is response to God expressed in their service to others.

Finally, ministers who are participating in, and are helping

their people to participate in, the correlation between questions
and answers will learn from doing. Many seminary teachers
are concerned because of the decline of study habits on the
part of their graduates. Evidence indicates that unless books
are a resource to the dialogue during the time of their training, many graduates lose interest in reading and disciplined
study because of the new and absorbing interest in their work.
They find the books that they studied remote from life, and
life uninformed by the books. This is not a judgment on the
students but on the educators, who were not trained to learn
from their work and who did not learn that their theology
books had something to say concerning the meaning of work.
This failure to correlate thought and action is a disastrous fault
in any education but especially so in the education of men who
represent Christ and His gift to the world. It is possible to
train for the ministry so that they will become better students
rather than worse. They can be trained to reflect upon, study,
and learn from their life and work and be driven to their books
for help in understanding what they do. The books may
illumine the work and the work raise the question that opens
the book.

C. *For post-ordination training*

The next recommendations have to do with the post-ordination training of ministers. The vast majority of graduates of
seminaries never again receive any kind of intensive training
for their work. A few are able to engage in graduate study, and
many attend clergy conferences of one kind or another. Most
clergy conferences, however, seem to be primarily concerned
with subject-matter presentations which certainly help to keep
clergy informed. But such conferences, because of both restricted time and method, do not meet the depth of need that

ministers have. Both the evaluation of the conferences and the statements of the clergy indicate clearly that some kind of follow-up training after a period of service in the ministry is wanted in which they have opportunity to share their questions and problems, to rethink their theology, and in general to receive help in learning from their experience in the ministry.

1. Extension departments for seminaries

Seminaries might develop, as they are able, extension departments for their graduates. If the need was to be met, this would mean that a full-time department would have to be provided whose sole responsibility would be for the advanced training program. The department would need a director to organize and conduct the course. It would be essential that the members of the faculty take their turns in meeting with these small groups of men, who, out of their ministry, would raise their questions. This would provide the teachers with a feed-back on the results of their courses.

Even if pre-ordination training were adequate, post-ordination training would be needed to further that which was begun in the seminaries. And the more inadequate seminary training remains, the more post-ordination training is needed. After a period of three or four years in the ministry, young ministers are ready for additional training and help. They know firsthand what the ministry is like. They now know what some of their assets and liabilities are. They know what are some of the problems of the parish and community life. They are open to an education that could not be given them before they were ordained.

In brief, this kind of program would strengthen and renew the younger ministry of the Church, and would reform and revitalize the theological education of each new generation of ministers.

2. Teacher training in graduate centers

The second recommendation, addressed to the graduate centers where the teachers for our seminaries are mainly prepared, is that along with the emphasis on the training of graduate students in content mastery, an equal stress be given training for teaching. Is it not inconsistent for so-called Christian teachers to brag that they know nothing about teaching as some have been heard to do? Future teachers should not only be checked on their scholarship but also on their ability to teach people. Some men are naturally great teachers and might be spoiled by a self-conscious consideration of the teaching relationship. On the other hand, many men do not have the natural gifts of a teacher and do not find the true grace for it as easily. They should have help in learning the art and science of communication. If they truly aspire to be Christian teachers, they will submit to this discipline with becoming humility. If this were done, there might be a little less arrogance among theological educators, who, in some instances, because of their sense of superiority and lack of relevance, have done the Protestant ministry, and therefore the Protestant Church, serious and lasting disservice. The evidence of this is written in the lives and the ministry of their graduates, the tragic results of which overflow into their personal lives and the lives of their families.

It is hard for human institutions to submit to judgment, especially when they have met with a kind of success. Truly great is the institution which in the face of its acceptance as a place of learning can bring its program under the kind of critical appraisal that challenges its personnel. The question therefore is, can these institutions prepare the Church's teachers, not only in the disciplines of study but also in the arts of teaching?

3. *Denominational schools for clergy*

The third recommendation urges the denominations to develop, as they are able, advanced programs of training for their own clergy. Presbyterians [1] under their Division of Christian Education have already made a significant start. They are completing an experiment in the conduct of a school for young pastors from which they hope to develop an advanced program of training for their younger ministers. Other denominations are in various stages of study of the same problem and it is hoped that they will persist in their efforts to meet the need for the continuing education of their clergy.

4. *The need for special resources*

The final recommendation concerns the development of special agencies that might contribute to the advanced training of ministers. The College of Preachers [2] already has an illustrious history of service to the ministers of the Episcopal Church in the work of preaching. The Institute of Religion [3] and the Institute for Advanced Pastoral Studies [4] are two other illustrations of the kind of resources that may be developed to help men in their further preparation for the Church's ministry. So likewise have the Council for Clinical Training,[5] the Institute of Pastoral Care,[6] and the American Foundation of Religion and Psychiatry [7] made notable contributions to the

[1] Dr. Lewis A. Briner, Board of Christian Education, United Presbyterian Church, Witherspoon Building, Philadelphia 7, Pennsylvania.

[2] The College of Preachers, Mount St. Alban, Washington 9, D.C.

[3] The Institute of Religion, Texas Medical Center, Houston, Texas.

[4] Institute for Advanced Pastoral Studies, Bloomfield Hills, Michigan.

[5] Council for Clinical Training, Inc., 2 East 103rd Street, New York 29, N.Y.

[6] Institute of Pastoral Care, Inc., P.O. Box 57, Worcester, Massachusetts.

[7] American Foundation of Religion and Psychiatry, 3 West 29th Street, New York 1, N.Y.

training of ministers. There are others too numerous to mention here. But care should be taken to make sure that the program offered meets the needs of ministers and not the needs of those offering the courses!

The concluding word is that post-ordination training, or "continuing" theological education as it is sometimes called, provides us with a leadership training opportunity that is greatly needed and that we should take seriously. Not only will the education of our clergy be continued but clues will also be given for the training of seminary students. Dare we accept this opportunity to break the stereotypes of theological education?